Which Greek Text?

The Debate Among Fundamentalists

Charles L. Surrett

Surrett Family Publications

Kings Mountain, NC

Second Printing, 2013

ISBN 978-0-9789331-0-4

Acknowledgments

Three acknowledgments must be made at the outset of this work. First, it is important to acknowledge that I, as the author, make no claim to be a qualified textual critic. Although I have done some secondary research of the comments of textual critics, I have not personally investigated ancient manuscripts to make my own comparisons. I rely heavily upon the observations of others.

Second, I acknowledge the help of individuals who have proof-read my work, at various stages of the process, to offer advice and suggestions. Among these are Dr. James Qurollo, Dr. David Cloud, Dr. Thomas Strouse, Mr. Ken Sheets, and Dr. Clifford Clark. Also, among my colleagues on the faculty of Ambassador Baptist College, Mr. Joel Spencer, Mr. Frank Camp, and Mrs. Mary Rosenau have all helped. The mention of names here should not be construed as an endorsement of this book by those individuals, but I took suggestions from several of them that resulted in changes in this text. Dr. Alton Beal has been an encouragement, particularly in the design of the cover for this booklet. Special appreciation must be expressed to the individual who proof-read it at *every* stage and spent the most time in the process — my precious wife, Rosanne.

Third, I want to acknowledge the encouragement of the dear people of the church which I was privileged to serve as pastor — Emmanuel Independent Baptist of Kings Mountain, North Carolina. Thank you, dear friends and co-workers.

Chuck Surrett

Table of Contents

Glossary of Terms

Autographa = The original writings of David, Paul, etc.

Canonization = The churches' stamp of approval upon the books accepted as Scripture.

Conflation = Theory that assumes a given MS combines the readings of two earlier MSS.

Critical Text = Westcott and Hort's text of 1881.

Dynamic Equivalency = Translation philosophy that adds editorial commentary to explain the sense.

Eclectic = Choosing parts from various texts.

Extant = Manuscripts that have been discovered.

Formal Equivalency = Translation philosophy that attempts to follow the same form as the original.

Majuscules = Earliest MSS written in all capital letters (also called Uncials).

Manuscript = Partial or complete copies of the autographa.

Miniscules = Later MSS, small letters (also called Cursives).

Preservation = The accessability of every word of Scripture for every generation of mankind.

Traditional Text = The primary Greek text used throughout church history. Also called "Syrian," "Byzantine,", or "*Textus Receptus*."

Versions = Translations of the Bible.

Abbreviations

CT = Critical Text (identical or similar to W-H Text)

KJV = King James Version

MS = Manuscript (Singular)

MSS = Manuscripts (Plural)

MT = Masoretic Text (Hebrew Old Testament)

NASV = New American Standard Version

NIV = New International Version

TEV = Today's English Version

TR = *Textus Receptus*

W-H = Westcott and Hort Text (Critical Text)

Chapter 1

What's the Big Problem?

In Bible-believing circles a great controversy exists. The debate revolves around the reliability of the Scriptures. It is not the old Modernist-Fundamentalist controversy over the *inspiration* of Scripture, but rather a present-day debate over the *preservation* of Scripture. On the one hand, there are those who think that the Word of God has *not* been verbally preserved by God, at least not in one given text or translation. Some of these think that God *has* preserved His Word, but that all the extant manuscripts must be studied to discern where it is. In practice, since no one can consult all the manuscripts every time he translates from the Greek, this position denies preservation from the standpoint of *accessability.* On the other hand, there are those who think that God has not only preserved His Word, but that He preserved it in a specific English translation, which some would even call "inspired." There is yet another position (espoused here) which maintains that God *has* preserved the words of the original, inspired writings (also called "autographa") of Scripture, and that those words are now available in a given Hebrew text of the Old Testament and a given Greek text of the New Testament.

Those Bible-believers who do not think that the Bible has been preserved in any given text usually follow the Greek text of the New Testament published in 1881 by Westcott and Hort or else some more recent derivative of it. This Greek text has become the source for nearly all of the modern translations of the New Testament since that time. Those Bible-believers who think that God has preserved His Word in a specific English translation are normally referring to the King James Version, which was first published in 1611. However, the commonly-used KJV Bibles today are *not* identical with the 1611 edition, for they follow the 1769 revision made by Benjamin Blayney.[1] Some KJV proponents see this translation as being *inspired* in the same way that the original autographs were.

Those who believe in the preservation of the original autographs in a given text are typically looking to the Textus Receptus of 1598 for the New Testament and the Masoretic Text for the Old. There are some who have chosen to use the Majority Text for the New Testament, which was first published in 1982. Whereas the term "Majority Text" prior to 1982 referred to the Traditional Text, that same name was chosen for the 1982 publication of the text. As of this writing, there has not been an English translation of the 1982 text published.

The Traditional Text, also called the *Textus Receptus*, is published by the Trinitarian Bible Society, and comes through the editing work of Erasmus, Stephanus, Beza, the Elzivir brothers, and others from the sixteenth and seventeenth centuries A.D. Its prior historical roots are in what have been called the "Syrian," "Antiochian," or "Byzantine" textual tradition. Although the number of manuscripts grows with new archaeological findings, the latest number of known Greek manuscripts (MSS), either partial or complete, totals 5,656.[2] Of these, over 5,250 support the reading of the TR.[3] The earliest thus far discovered are traceable to the latter half of the fourth century A.D., as seen in the writings of Chrysostom and other church fathers from the area of Antioch in Syria

---

[1] W. Edward Glenny, in The Bible Version Debate: The Perspective of Central Baptist Theological Seminary (Minneapolis: Central Baptist Theological Seminary, 1997), 59.

[2] Ibid., 42.

[3] Ibid.

(where Paul's missionary journeys started). The introduction to the Westcott-Hort Greek text declares that there has been no significant change in the "Syrian" or "Byzantine" text-types since then.[4] The earliest forms of this text that have been discovered, then, were probably produced at least 250 years after the writing of the Revelation by the Apostle John.

The Critical Text, also called "eclectic," is published by the United Bible Societies, represents primarily the work of Westcott and Hort, and first appeared in 1881. It is based largely on three "families" of ancient texts, called "Western," "Alexandrian," and "Neutral." Where these differ from each other, the "Alexandrian" strain was most often considered by W-H to be best. Far fewer MSS have been found to support this position, but they are purported to be older than the Syrian strain, with the two chief MSS being **B** *(Vaticanus)* and ***Aleph*** *(Sinaiticus)*, which are thought to have originated in the third century (more than 100 years after the original writing of the Revelation). This smaller group of texts not only differs significantly from the "Syrian" texts, but they also differ considerably from each other.[5]

A comparison of the two major Greek texts is recorded by Thomas M. Strouse:

> The *textus receptus* has 140,521 Greek words. The *textus criticus* changes (primarily by adding or subtracting) 9,970 Greek words. This results in a

---

[4] Brooke Foss Westcott and John Anthony Hort, The New Testament in the Original Greek (New York: the MacMillan Company, 1928), 546-547.

[5] Wilbur Pickering, The Identity of the New Testament Text (Nashville: Thomas Nelson Publishers, 1977), 16.

7% difference between the CT and the TR. Thus, the TR and the CT are identical with respect to 93% of their words.[6]

Strouse further notes that textual critics thus seem to agree that God has preserved 93% of His Word for man today, leaving many Fundamentalists in the position of accepting *"partial preservation."*[7] It is typical for advocates of the TR position to espouse *complete preservation* of God's Word.

In order for real progress to be made in the debate over versions, one must ascertain the proper *level* at which investigation should be made. It is asserted here that the level of translations is *not* at the heart of the issue. Since every major English translation of the Scripture charges readers with the dangers of "adding to" or "taking away from" its words, each translation claims its own accuracy, to the exclusion of all others. Thus, the mere exposure of differences in translation proves nothing by itself, for each of the compared translations simply condemns all of the others, leaving no real solution to the problem. Nor is it fair to charge them with teaching heretical doctrines, based on the limited comparison of one verse in one translation with the same verse in another. For example, the modern versions have been assailed for "denying" either the blood or the Deity of Jesus Christ, by comparing their wordings with that of the KJV in selected passages. However, the only way to prove that any version actually denies such doctrines would be to carefully study its renditions of the *hundreds* of passages that deal with those subjects. If the

---

6 Thomas M. Strouse, Fundamentalism and the Authorized Version, (Virginia Beach, VA: Tabernacle Baptist Theological Press, 1996), 4.

7 *Ibid.*, 6.

blood of Christ is *never* seen to be crucial for man's salvation, or if Jesus is *never* presented as God, then the accusations would seem to be fair. However, that is not the case with the popular modern versions (such as NASVand NIV), for such doctrines can clearly be found in them.

The inspiration of Scriptures applies to the original autographs (those writings in Hebrew, Aramaic, and Greek of Moses, Daniel, Paul, and others), of which, because of physical deterioration over the years, none is existent today. The fairest debate is over which original language *texts* best represent the originals, not over their *translations* into other languages. The biggest reason for the divergence in *translations* of the Bible is the divergence in *texts used in those translations*, particularly in the New Testament. In other words, a translation may be well-done, but if it translates inferior Greek texts, it will be automatically flawed.

Another reason why one must look beyond the translation level to fairly deal with this issue has to do with the matter of the preservation of the Scriptures. Either the Word of God *has* been preserved by God for every generation of Church history, or it *has not*. Those who believe that the best Greek MSS were lost to Christianity for many centuries (W-H proponents) evidently do not think that God has preserved His Word for each generation. On the other hand, those who think that the KJV 1611 is an "inspired" translation that "corrects the Greek" evidently do not believe that God has preserved His Word for each generation either. While they may espouse the idea of preservation since 1611, they have a serious problem with church history prior to 1611. If all that the local churches possessed were corrupted copies of the Greek, then there may have been many centuries (and many more generations) which had no access to the "pure" words of God before the production of the KJV. In addition to being in error regarding the doctrine of the *inspiration* of Scripture, they are also in error regarding the doctrine of the *preservation* of Scripture. Nor should the debate rage at the level of name-calling and character assassination. The mere fact that a preacher or an author can string together a long list of derogatory adjectives to describe his opponents should not be taken as proof of his position. The sin nature of man is such that he seldom listens to the logic of an opponent who has insulted him. For example, those who call homosexuals "queers" are not very likely to win them to the Lord. If one truly desires to *edify* and *persuade* others to agree with him, he must use Biblical constraint in the manner of his presentation. The admonition of II Tim 2:24-25 is appropriate here:

> And the servant of the Lord must not strive; but be gentle unto all *men*, apt to teach, patient, In meekness instructing those that oppose themselves; if God peradventure will give them repentance to the acknowledging of the truth. . . .

Those who defend the TR and the KJV have been considered "ignorant," "unscholarly," and "out of touch with reality." Those who take the opposite position have been called "compromisers," "hypocrites," and "heretics." This kind of rhetoric adds plenty of heat to the debate, but very little light. Rather than erecting theological "straw men" and then blowing them down, it would seem far more profitable to discuss real *issues* like real *Christians* should.

It will not be the scope of this study to deal with the Old Testament Hebrew; consequently nothing further will be said of the Masoretic Text. The basic principles used to prefer the TR can also be applied to the selection of the MT. Also, since the 1982 Majority Text proponents follow essentially the same line of reasoning as do those who use the Textus Receptus, there will not be an attempt here to defend the choice of the TR over the 1982 text. The bulk of this study will focus upon the choice of the Greek text of the Textus Receptus (TR) over that of the Westcott and Hort (W-H) tradition. As for those who consider themselves "King James only," the subject of translations will be briefly addressed.

This is not a study that separates Fundamentalists from Liberals, for all of the above-mentioned views are held by individuals who consider themselves to be Fundamentalists. This is being written from the viewpoint of a Fundamentalist Independent Baptist, and it is expected that the majority of readers will also fit that description. At any rate, it is important that a Biblical attitude be maintained by all who consider this issue. May the principles of the following Scriptural admonitions be carefully followed: "Let not him that eateth despise him that eateth not; and let not him which eateth not judge him that eateth. . . . (See Rom 14:1-6)." ". . . Endeavouring to keep the unity of the Spirit in the bond of peace (Eph 4:3)." "But the wisdom that is from above is first pure, then peaceable, gentle, *and* easy to be intreated, full of mercy and good fruits, without partiality, and without hypocrisy (Js 3:17)."

Chapter 2

Evolution and Textual Criticism

There seems to be a parallel between the integration of Darwinian evolutionary thought into the theology of committed Bible-believers of the late nineteenth and early twentieth centuries with that of the acceptance of Westcott-Hort at the same period in history. The mood, especially in Europe and North America, favored scientific investigation as an ultimate source of truth. The Liberals capitalized on this "modern" way of thinking to produce what has become known as Higher Criticism. Fundamentalists rejected those Liberal conclusions, but still felt the need to accommodate what they thought were the findings of science. In the area of Creationism, Bible-believers replaced the long-held view of six literal days of creation with some type of evolutionary explanation, such as the "Day-Age" or the "Gap" theory. Christians today do not castigate the late C. I. Scofield nor doubt either his salvation or sincerity on the basis of his Gap Theory beliefs of creation. Simply put, he and others like him did not have the information to combat what they thought were conclusions forced by science and scholarship. With the subsequent work of Whitcomb and Morris, for example, there is confidence today that the long-standing, orthodox view of creation is the right one. It is now clear that the position held by local churches for centuries on the origin of the Universe is, in fact, the right one.

Perhaps the debate on the textual issue will bring to light information that persuades Fundamentalism that the long-standing, widely-accepted text was actually the best one after all. If such occurs, one need not judge that those who accepted conclusions which they thought were forced by science and scholarship were either heretics or hypocrites. In fact, many are Godly men of great academic abilities, who also have an abiding commitment to the accuracy and authority of the Scriptures.

The basic position of the W-H theory of textual transmission involves the fact that their body of texts was hidden from the public for about fourteen centuries of Church history. The early manuscripts (MSS) to which Westcott and Hort gave the greatest credence were not available for general use from the fourth century until the nineteenth. Thus, the W-H concept presents a textual "Gap Theory" as its foundation. This, of course, denies that God's Word has been available for every generation of mankind.

The attitude of Christian tolerance ought to characterize people on *both* sides of these issues. Although the textual *position* of Dr. Stewart Custer will be rejected here, the Godly *disposition* which he espouses is highly commendable:

> The real question which must be settled is which type of text most closely reflects the wording of the original. Good men may disagree on this question without automatically becoming heretics or apostates.[8]

While some might think it is a compromising spirit that allows one to be charitable in this debate, it must be remembered that, whereas *our* Bible and the Greek text underlying it both warn against "adding to" or "taking away from" its words, so do *their* Bible(s) and their underlying Greek text. Thus, *some form of textual criticism* (evaluation of the texts) is necessary, in order to know which text truly deserves our loyalty. For the New Testament, the *Textus Receptus* (TR) best represents God's preserved Word.

---

[8]Stewart Custer, The Truth About the King James Version Controversy (Greenville: Bob Jones University Press, Inc., 1981), 8-9.

Comparison of W-H With Darwinism

The Theory	Darwinism	W-H Theory
Year	1859	1881
Manner of Presentation	Series of guesses, stated in the form of over 600 hypothetical statements	Frequent use of terms like "conjecture," "probabilities," "presumptions," "suppositions," etc.
Conclusion of followers	Scientific/historic fact, with virtually no reason to reject.	Scientific/histori c fact, with virtually no reason to reject.
How presented in classrooms	The findings of science	The "oldest and best" MSS
Reaction of many conservative Bible-believers	Assume it to be proved, and adapt creationism to include some form of it ("Gap," etc)	Assume it to be proved and change Greek texts and translations used
Reaction to contrary evidence	Reject Darwins's reasons, but maintain his conclusions.	Reject W-H's reasons but maintain their conclusions.
Reaction of believers	Reject Darwin and return to Creationism	Reject W-H and return to view of traditional believers.

Chapter 3

Preservation: the "Watershed" Issue

There is one central issue that divides the two sides of the debate over the TR versus the W-H text. Even a cursory study of textual criticism brings one to discover that the real "watershed" issue among Fundamentalists is whether or not God has promised to preserve His Word in an accessible form for every generation of believers.

There seems to be little value in finding fault with such men as Origen, Chrysostom, Erasmus, King James, John Burgon, or Westcott and Hort. In point of fact, no matter which textual tradition is accepted, one must in some way go through the Roman Catholic and Anglican denominations to find the text. One either basically depends upon the work of Erasmus, who was a Catholic priest, or the tradition that places greatest authority in **B**, the text discovered in the Vatican. It is also true that the principle disputers of the issue (Burgon, Westcott, and Hort) were all Anglicans. Since some writers of the original autographa were blasphemers, persecutors, murderers, liars, adulterers, and Christ-deniers, it is obvious that the integrity of the Bible does not depend upon the integrity of the human vessels through whom it was transported. If that is true of the originals, it must also be true of the copies. In fact, no matter which textual tradition is taken as best, it has gone through dirty hands at many levels. This is not a problem for those who attribute the accuracy of the Bible to the integrity of the God Who promised to preserve it. It does, however, lead a proponent of the W-H text to say, "We do not believe that God has perfectly preserved His Word by miraculous, supernatural means in any one manuscript, version, or text-type."[9]

He further clarifies this by saying,

> . . . It is better to say He has preserved His Word in and through the thousands of extant manuscripts, and that those who seek truth must compare those manuscripts to determine the correct readings when the manuscripts differ.[10]

Another proponent of the Critical Text offers this explanation:

> . . . The truth of infallibility does not extend to the preservation of an infallible text, nor to an infallible lexicography, nor to infallible answers to all questions about authorship, date, sources, etc., nor to an infallible reconstruction of the historical situation in which revelatory events occurred and the books of the Bible were written. Such questions God in His providence has committed to human scholarship to answer; and often the answers must be imperfect and tentative.[11]

---

[9] Glenny, 71.

[10] Ibid, 78.

[11] George Eldon Ladd, <u>The New Testament and Criticism</u> (Grand Rapids: William B. Eerdmans Publishing Company, 1983), 217.

Fundamentalists would do well to question whether God places such a premium upon "human scholarship." The low view of Westcott and Hort themselves concerning God's preservation of the text can be seen from some of their own statements in the introduction to their text:

> In the fourth century mixture prevailed almost everywhere: nearly all its texts, so far as they can be seen through the quotations of theologians, are more or less chaotic. In the early years the persecution under Diocletian and his colleagues, and then the reaction under Constantine, must have affected the text not less powerfully than the Canon of the New Testament.[12]

Opponents of the W-H theory would question their assumption that canonization "affected" the text. It seems more in keeping with Church history to acknowledge that canonization *verified* the text that was already accepted, rather than *affecting* it.

Further demonstration of the rejection of the Divine preservation of Scripture is seen in the following statements of Westcott and Hort: "Apart from miscellaneous and accidental mixture, it is probable that more than one eclectic text was deliberately formed."[13]

> When the Western text was growing up . . . the reverence paid to the writings which ultimately

[12] Westcott and Hort, 552.

[13] Ibid, 551.

formed the Canon of the New Testament had not yet assumed a character that would forbid what might well seem their temperate enrichment from other memories or records. [14]

". . . Unless the reading is such as can naturally be accounted for by accidental coincidence . . . ."[15] "But it is at least theoretically possible that the originality of the text thus attained is relative only, and that all existing documents are affected by errors introduced in the early stages of transmission."[16] "Wherever it has appeared to the editors, or to either of them, that the text probably contains some primitive error, that is, has not been quite rightly preserved in any existing document. . . ."[17]

Those who believe in the preservation of the text by God find the above statements reprehensible. It appears that the text of Scripture, if treated in the W-H fashion, would then have a large number of uncertainties, either by accident or deliberate action. Whatever the cause or motive, such uncertainties deny the concept of the Providential preservation of the text of Scripture.

---

[14] Ibid, 557.

[15] Ibid, 558.

[16] Ibid, 563.

[17] Ibid, 583.

Chapter 4

Uncertainties of W-H Theory

Very recently, followers of the W-H tradition of texts have tried to distance themselves somewhat from the originators. The new mode of thinking considers the modern translations, like NIV and NASV, to be based on an "eclectic" text, rather than W-H. This is due to a current reaction against the flaws in the W-H theory by those who yet follow the W-H conclusions.[18] Cloud reacts to this reasoning by producing the following evidence of the similarity between recently-produced texts with that of Westcott and Hort:

> The fact is that the United Bible Societies (UBS) text is almost identical to the W-H text of 1881 *in significant departures from the Received Text.* For example, both the W-H and the UBS delete or question almost the same number of verses (WH--48, UBS--45). Both delete almost the same number of significant portions of verses (WH--193, UBS 185). Both delete almost the same number of names and titles of the Lord (WH--221, UBS--212). An extensive comparison of the TR against the WH text, the Nestle's Text, the UBS text, and Key English versions was done by the late Everett Fowler and can be seen in his book *Evaluating Versions of the New Testament,* available from Bible for Today.
>
> The W-H text of 1881 and the latest edition

---

[18] David W. Cloud, editor, "O Timothy Magazine," volume 15, issues 3-4, 1998, 33.

> of the United Bible Societies' text differ only in relatively minor points. Both represent the same TYPE of text with the same TYPE of departures from the Received Text.
>
> The fact is that the Westcott-Hort text represents the first widely-accepted departure from the TR in the post-Reformation era, and the modern English versions descend directly from it.[19]

Westcott and Hort, the primary craftsmen of modern textual criticism, have expressed doubts about the accuracy of their product, as can be seen in the following quotations from the introduction to their Greek New Testament: ". . . The imperfection of our knowledge more commonly leaves unreconciled the apparent conflict of the two kinds of probability. . . ."[20]

> That is what is meant when it is said in popular language that "good MSS" should be trusted. A presumption of relatively high authority is conferred by priority of date; a presumption verified on the average by experience, but still no more than a presumption. . . .[21]

"On the other hand the inequalities and occasional ambiguities in the evidence for the genealogical relations

---

[19] Ibid., 33-34.

[20] Westcott and Hort, 542.

[21] Ibid., 543.

frequently leave room for more than one interpretation."[22]

"But all these drawbacks, however they introduce ambiguity into the evidence for single passages. . . ."[23]

> Numerous variations remain in which the distribution of documentary evidence may be reasonably interpreted in more ways than one, so that a reference of the several readings to this or that principal ancient text is open to doubt. . . .[24]
>
> If **B** and ***Aleph*** were for a great part of their text derived from a proximate common original, that common original, whatever might have been its own date, must have had a very ancient and a very pure text. There is however no tangible evidence for this supposition. . . .[25]
>
> Even when **B** stands quite alone, its readings must never be lightly rejected, though here full account has to be taken of the chances of clerical error . . . . On the other hand the readings in which ***Aleph*** stands alone bear almost always the marks of either carelessness or boldness. . . .[26]

---

[22] Ibid., 546-547.

[23] Ibid., 547.

[24] Ibid., 557.

[25] Ibid., 559.

[26] Ibid., 560.

"The wrong readings of **B** . . . being for the most part due only to sporadic corruptions. . . ."[27]

> Although however a text formed by taking **B** as the sole authority . . . would certainly include many wrong readings: and the only safe criticism is that which throughout takes account of all existing evidence.[28]

> Whether **B** ever contained the Apocalypse or not, it is now defective from Hebrews ix 14 onward. The loss is the greater because in the Apocalypse ***Aleph*** has a text conspicuously inferior to its text of the other books, partly inherited from earlier more or less corrupted texts . . . it does but imperfectly supply the deficiency. . . .[29]

"Genealogical results . . . supply the presumptions, stronger or weaker as the case may be, which constitute the primary and often the virtually decisive evidence for one reading as against another."[30]

> No definite rule can be given in the comparatively few cases in which the apparent conflict remains. . . . The ultimate determination must evidently be here

---

[27] Ibid., 561.

[28] Ibid., 561.

[29] Ibid., 562.

[30] Ibid., 563.

> left to personal judgement. . . . Here, as in the many variations in which documentary and internal evidence are both indecisive, it is manifestly right to abstain from placing before the reader an appearance of greater certainty than really exists. . . to mark the places where an absolute decision would at present be arbitrary. . . .[31]

"There are however some passages which one or both of us suspect to contain a primitive error of no great importance. . . ."[32] "The expression of doubt wherever doubt is really felt is owing to the paramount necessity for fidelity as to the exact words of Scripture."[33]

> Wherever it has been found impossible to decide that one of two or more various readings is certainly right, alternative readings are given: and no alternative reading is given which does not appear to have a reasonable probability of being the true reading.[34]

"On the other hand the inequalities and occasional ambiguities in the evidence for the genealogical relations

---

[31] Ibid., 563.

[32] Ibid., 564.

[33] Ibid., 565.

[34] Ibid., 581.

frequently leave room for more than one interpretation."[35]

It is obvious from the quotations above that the compilers of the W-H text did not think that they had reproduced the inerrant Word of God. They did not even have much confidence in **B**, which is also called ***Vaticanus***, or ***Aleph***, which is ***Sinaiticus***, the two main sources from which they drew their text. Nor do they claim to have a good text of the entire Book of the Revelation, which appears to undermine the Word of God. They should be commended, however, for restraint and honesty in their presentation. The frequent usage of terms such as "conjecture," "probabilities," "presumptions," "ambiguity," "suppositions," *etc.*, are a fair way of avoiding the sin of over-statement that has often clouded debate over these issues. Such honesty would serve well both those who agree and those who disagree with Westcott and Hort.

Nevertheless, the uncertainties of W-H are largely due to their rejection of the vast majority of extant MSS, which they refer to as the "Syrian" text. Their reasons for this rejection have been summarized as follows:

> 1. This text goes back to a revision of the Greek text in the 4th century, probably under the leadership of Lucianus of Antioch;
> 2. This text can on external grounds be characterized as a late text: it is not found in the old majuscules and it is not followed by the Church Fathers before Nicea in their New Testament

---

[35] Ibid., 546-547.

> quotations;
> 3. This text can on internal grounds be characterized as secondary because of its inclusive nature (conflate readings) and because of its tendency to harmonize and assimilate, leading to a complete and lucid text.[36]

Van Bruggen offers a thoughtful rebuttal to the W-H prejudice against the Traditional Text:

> . . . We can say that the large number of manuscripts wherein the traditional or Church text occurs, must carry weight. This striking number can not be disqualified with an appeal . . . about Lucianus of Antioch. It also can not be put aside as meaningless, as though it is to be traced back to one archetype in the 4th century. On the contrary, the large number deserves attention, since, in the midst of all sorts of variation, it confronts us with a growing uniformity. It rather points in the direction of a simultaneous turning-back in various centres (*sic*) to the same central point of the original text.[37]

---

[36] Jakob Van Bruggen, The Ancient Text of the New Testament (Winnipeg: Premier Printing, Ltd., 1976), 15.

[37] Ibid., 21.

Chapter 5

Further Uncertainties

Individuals who have produced Greek texts patterned after W-H and some of those who have translated from this "family" of Greek texts have also expressed uncertainty about their work.

Erwin Nestle and Kurt Aland produced a text entitled Novum Testamentum Graece in 1960. This text was the twenty-fourth edition of their work. It was based upon a similar work by Eberhard Nestle, Erwin's father, who had also followed W-H. For those who wonder what confidence Erwin Nestle had in his product, the following quotations should be instructive: "The number of these further readings was increased with successive impressions and important conjectures were also added."[38]

> Thus the text, built up on the work of the 19th century, has remained as a whole unchanged, particularly since the research of recent years has not yet led to the establishment of a generally acknowledged N.T. text.[39]
>
> In addition, there are now included . . . most of the variations in the Gospels (with the exception of

---

[38] Erwin Nestle and Kurt Aland, eds., Novum Testamentum Graece (Stuttgart, Germany: Wurttembergischen Bibelenstalt Stuttgart, 24th edition, 1960), 60.

[39] Ibid., 62.

> some transpositions and other not very important divergences which had to be omitted through lack of space. . . .[40]

"The number of conjectures taken up has been multiplied . . . *cj*=conjecit has been added where a radical alteration of the traditional spelling is concerned (Mt 7,15)."[41] "These conjectures stand in brackets, to distinguish them from the readings handed down in manuscripts. Altogether there have been entered about 200 conjectures, with 90 names of authors."[42]

> With this selection of material offered, at least some wishes will remain unsatisfied; but at any rate some material should be proffered, in the space at our disposal, for use in lectures, and to stimulate individual study.[43]

"Thus, Mt 4,9 . . . few or no witnesses besides, agree with our text. . . ."[44] "That there is always somewhat of an uncertainty in these inferences, has already been remarked."[45] "Occasionally parts of words not in the

---

40 Ibid., 66.

41 Ibid., 67.

42 Ibid.

43 Ibid.

44 Ibid., 78.

45 Ibid., 79.

tradition but only surmised, have been enclosed in square brackets. . . ."[46] "(***A special symbol***) stands where a quotation is to be presumed, but where no source is known. . . ."[47]

It is again commendable that the editor is honest about his conclusions, and particularly noteworthy that he wanted his work "to stimulate further study." One wonders how many college and seminary students and their professors see the text in this way and do further study to see if it is accurate. Regarding the W-H small edition, from which he drew so heavily, Nestle made the following statements:

". . . On account of their good attestation they have taken up into the text or margin, but which nevertheless because of their bad sense aroused manifest doubts in them. . . ."[48]

> (***A specific symbol***) . . . means that this passage did indeed appear doubtful to them, but that they did not wish to give the preference to any other reading. . . . Where they did not approve any traditional reading, but made a conjecture, this is designated by . . . (***another specific symbol***), when both make the conjecture, e.g. Act 12,25, and by . . . (***yet another specific symbol***) when only one does so, as

[46] Ibid.

[47] Ibid., 81.

[48] Ibid., 77.

Mt 28,7.[49]

Kurt Aland was involved in the production of another Greek New Testament, this time with the assistance of Matthew Black, Bruce Metzger, and Allen Wikgren, published in 1966. These editors also gave statements that describe the level of confidence they had in their work, as seen in the introduction:

". . . The Greek text was established, the degree of certainty for the reading adopted in the text was estimated . . . ."[50] "It is the intention of the committee from time to time to revise its work in order to take into account new discoveries and fresh evidence."[51] "Square brackets are used to enclose words which are regarded as having dubious textual validity."[52]

> Double square brackets are used to enclose passages which are regarded as later additions to the text, but which are retained because of their evident antiquity and their importance in the textual tradition.[53]

---

[49] Ibid.

[50] Kurt Aland, Matthew Black, Bruce M. Metzger, and Allen Wikgren, editors, The Greek New Testament (Stuttgart: Wurttemberg Bible Society, 1966), vi.

[51] Ibid., vii.

[52] Ibid., x.

[53] Ibid., x.

> By means of the letters A, B, C, and D, enclosed within "braces" { } at the beginning of each set of textual variants, the Committee has sought to indicate the relative degree of certainty . . . for the reading adopted as the text. The letter A signifies that the text is virtually certain, while B indicates that there is some degree of doubt. The letter C means that there is considerable degree of doubt . . . while D shows that there is a very high degree of doubt concerning the reading selected for the text.[54]

> Furthermore, the manuscripts of the Church Fathers have suffered the usual transcriptional modifications to which all ancient manuscripts were subject; this was especially true for Biblical passages where the tendency of scribes was to accommodate readings to the Byzantine textual tradition.[55]

Not only the textual editors, but also some of those who have translated from their texts, have expressed questions about the accuracy of the preservation of God's Word. The preface to the Revised Standard Version gives the following observations: "Many difficulties and obscurities, of course, remain."[56]

If in the judgment of the Committee the meaning of

---

[54] Ibid., x-xi.

[55] Ibid., xxx.

[56] Preface to the Revised Standard Version (New York: Thomas Nelson & Sons, 1953), vi.

a passage is quite uncertain or obscure, either because of corruption in the text or because of the inadequacies of our present knowledge of the language, that fact is indicated by a note. It should not be assumed, however, that the Committee was entirely sure or unanimous concerning every rendering not so indicated.[57]

The present publication has afforded the Committee opportunity to review its work and to consider criticisms and suggestions from various readers. As a result, about eighty changes are made in the present edition.[58]

Departures from the consonantal text of the best manuscripts have been made only where it seems clear that errors in copying had been made before the text was standardized. Most of the corrections adopted are based on the ancient versions. . . .[59]

Sometimes it is evident that the text has suffered in transmission, but none of the versions provides a satisfactory restoration. Here we can only follow the best judgment of competent scholars as to the most probable reconstruction of the original text.[60]

---

[57] Ibid., vi.

[58] Ibid., viii.

[59] Ibid., v.

[60] Ibid.

"To achieve clarity the translators sometimes supplied words not in the original texts but required by the context. If there was uncertainty about such material, it is enclosed in brackets."[61]

The editors of the New International Version of 1980 have given similar statements indicating their uncertainty: "Readings from these versions were occasionally followed where the Masoretic Text seemed doubtful. . . . "[62] "Footnotes call attention to places where there was uncertainty about what the original text was."[63] "As in other ancient documents, the precise meaning of the biblical texts is sometimes uncertain."[64] "In some cases two possible translations were considered to have about equal validity."[65]

The critical textual position, with all its uncertainties, produces a logical dilemma for its advocates. A respected theologian who accepted the W-H position, B. B. Warfield, said:

> The best the press can do is measurably to stop the growth of corruption and faithfully to perpetuate all that has already grown. No wonder that the current

---

[61] Ibid., xii.

[62] Preface to The Holy Bible: New International Version (Grand Rapids: Zondervan Bible Publishers, 1980), x.

[63] Ibid.

[64] Ibid., xi.

[65] Ibid., xiii.

> New Testament text must be adjudged, in comparison with a well printed modern book, extremely corrupt.
>
> On the other hand, if we compare the present state of the New Testament text with that of any other ancient writing, we must render the opposite verdict, and declare it to be marvellously (*sic*) correct. . . . such has been the providence of God in preserving for His Church in each and every age a competently exact text of the Scriptures. . . .[66]

It escapes the understanding of this writer how the Scripture could be Providentially preserved, "marvellously correct," "competently exact," and "extremely corrupt" all at the same time!

The above samplings are certainly not exhaustive, but clearly reveal that those who follow the W-H approach to the text of Scripture do not believe that God has Providentially preserved an accessible Greek text for every generation of mankind.

---

[66] Benjamin B. Warfield, An Introduction to the Textual Criticism of the New Testament (New York: Thomas Whittaker, 1886), 12.

Chapter 6

Biblical Evidence of Preservation

Logic demands the preservation of Scriptures. Verbal *inspiration* would fully benefit only the generation which originally received it, if there were not verbal *preservation* of that which was inspired. If man is accountable to God for *every word* of the Bible, then a just God must make available to mankind *every word* for which man is accountable. The following statement was written to prove the necessity of the *inspiration* of Scripture, but could just as well describe the necessity of its *preservation*:

> Without inspiration we could have no reliable revelation from God. . . .Words are the chief mode of human thought. They have specific meanings related to such factors as their derivation, their common usage, the geographical setting of their use, the time in which they are used, the subject matter under consideration, and their connotations. If God is to communicate with men, He must use the language of men. His message, therefore, could not be left to the thoughts and words of fallible human beings. Positive action by God was necessary to guarantee that the record conveyed the truth God intended.[67]

The same arguments could be forcibly used to

---

[67] Randolph Shaylor, editor, From the Mind of God to the Mind of Man, (Greenville: Ambassador-Emerald International, 1999), 17.

demand the *preservation* of the words that were given by inspiration. Why would God go to the "trouble" of breathing out words that were to be meticulously written down, if they were to be soon lost? There obviously is a logical inconsistency in rejecting "concept" *inspiration* while accepting "concept" *preservation.* Also, if God's Word has been preserved for man today, then careful exegesis of passages, with an emphasis on the precise meanings of words, is a rewarding activity. If not, then such precision is unnecessary.

However, the primary issue of concern is not logic, but the actual teaching of the Scriptures on the subject. The view that defends Biblical preservation is seen by some as having no Scriptural foundation:

> It is the same with the issue of the preservation of God's Word. We do not have a promise in God's Word that He will preserve it, let alone details about how He will preserve it. We have the historical evidence. The historical evidence demonstrates that God has wonderfully preserved His Word by means of all the manuscripts, versions, and copies of Scripture available to us. Furthermore, the historical evidence must be the basis for our textual decisions. . . . God has providentially preserved the text of Scripture through history so that none of its doctrinal content is lost or affected adversely. However, we need to remember that this conviction is not based on a verse of Scripture; it is based on the evidence of

history.[68]

However, let it also be considered that if God has not promised to preserve His Word, then there could conceivably have been a conspiracy in history to preserve only *corruptions* of God's Word, and Christians would be none the wiser today. Only if the Bible records a promise from God to preserve His Word can non-Biblical history be trusted to furnish evidence of that preservation. Furthermore, if history is to be the sole witness of the Bible's preservation, it would not point to the W-H text or any of its variations as that which has been best preserved for the most people and for the longest time. History points to the TR.

New Testament history records the preservation of the Old Testament, despite the fact that original manuscripts were then non-existent. Abraham said to the rich man, "They have Moses and the prophets. . . . (Lk 16:29)." Jesus told His contemporaries, "Search the scriptures . . . (Jn 5:39)." These statements seem to imply that the Word of God was readily available to individuals in NT times. In one of the classic passages about verbal inspiration (II Tim 3:16) there is evidence of preservation, for Timothy knew those scriptures from his early childhood (v 15). Fair hermeneutics would demand that the verbally-inspired scriptures of v 16 were identical in content with those scriptures which Timothy knew in v 15, despite the fact that different Greek words for "Scripture" were used in the two verses. Thus, even though Timothy did not have any

---

[68] Glenny, 94-95.

original Hebrew MSS, some of which had been written at least fifteen centuries earlier, he still had accurately-preserved copies that were precise duplications of that which had been "God-breathed." In another classic passage about inspiration (II Peter 1:21) there is again contextual evidence of preservation. In verse nineteen Peter said, "We have also a more sure word of prophecy; whereunto ye do well that ye take heed. . . ." Clearly, Peter and those to whom he wrote *had the Word of God in their possession*, despite the absence of the autographa.

The following New Testament references quote Old Testament passages, with the underlying assumption being that the text of the Old Testament had been preserved: Mt 21:42; Mk 12:10; 15:28; Lk 4:21; Jn 7:38,42; 13:18; 19:24,36,37; Acts 1:20; 8:32-33; Rom 4:3; 9:17; 10:11; 11:2-4; Gal 4:30; I Tim 5:18; Js 2:8,23; 4:5; I Pet 2:6. The following New Testament passages refer to the Old Testament scriptures, as if the text was available at the time of writing of the New Testament: Mt 22:29; 26:54,56; Mk 12:24; 14:49; Lk 24:27,32,45; Jn 5:39; 10:35; Acts 17:2,11; 18:24,28; Rom 1:2; 15:4; 16:26; I Cor 15:4; Gal 3:22; II Tim 3:15-16; I Pet 2:6; II Pet 1:19-20; 3:16.

While the above passages provide historical proof that the Old Testament had been preserved until the New Testament period, the Biblical evidence for preservation is strengthened by explicit statements which amount to God's promise to preserve His Word. There are many statements in Scripture to the effect that God's Word will be preserved for future (all) generations. Some examples are given here: Ps 33:11 -- "The counsel of the Lord standeth for ever . . . to all generations." Ps 100:5-- ". . . His truth *endureth* to all generations." The italicized word ("endureth") seems to be consistent with the intended meaning of this verse. Ps 111:7-8 -- ". . . All his commandments are sure. They stand fast for ever and ever. . . ." Ps 117:2-- ". . . And the truth of the Lord *endureth* for ever." Ps 119:89-90 -- "For ever, O LORD, thy word is settled in heaven. Thy faithfulness is unto all generations. . . ."

Since God is not in danger of forgetting what He said, this must mean that the Word is preserved for man's benefit. This seems to imply that God's Word is not only "settled in heaven," but also available on earth. Ps 119:144-- "The righteousness of thy testimonies is everlasting. . . ." This implies that the "testimonies" are also "everlasting." Ps 119:152 -- "Concerning thy testimonies, I have known of old that thou hast founded them for ever." The Hebrew word translated "founded" ". . . would signify something which cannot be moved."[69] Ps 119:160 -- "Thy word is true from the beginning: and every one of thy righteous judgments endureth for ever." Isa 40:8 -- ". . . The word of our God shall stand for ever." It has been proposed that this verse refers to only one specific promise (the return from captivity).[70] If so, does this promise "stand," as opposed to all other promises of God? Is the prophecy of return from captivity so theologically important that it must "stand" for centuries after its fulfillment and never be lost, while other theological ideas or words disappear? Since the passage

---

[69] Harris, Archer, and Waltke, eds., Theological Wordbook of the Old Testament (Chicago: Moody Press, 1980), vol 1, 384.

[70] Glenny, 89.

does not use the word, "promise," do we have a right to limit its meaning in this way? In reality, the Bible itself uses this passage for a broader application (see I Peter 1:25 below).

> Isa 59:21 -- "As for me, this is my covenant with them, saith the LORD; My spirit that is upon thee, and my words which I have put in thy mouth, shall not depart out of thy mouth, nor out of the mouth of thy seed, nor out of the mouth of thy seed's seed, saith the LORD, from henceforth and for ever."

Thus, *every generation* of God's people will have God's Word. Mt 5:18 -- ". . . Till heaven and earth pass, one jot or one tittle shall in no wise pass from the law, till all be fulfilled." Mt 24:35-- "Heaven and earth shall pass away, but my words shall not pass away." Lk 21:33 -- "Heaven and earth shall pass away: but my words shall not pass away." If it were not for the preservation of the *words* of Jesus in the Scripture, Bible students today would not know *what* He said, or even *if* He said anything at all! Jn 10:35 -- ". . . The scripture cannot be broken . . ." This does not mean that it cannot be disobeyed. It means it cannot be "destroyed," "brought to an end," "abolished," or "done away with."[71] Acts 7:38 -- ". . . Our fathers: who received the lively oracles to give unto us. . . ." The "fathers" referred to hearkened back to Moses' day, but passed the "living word" to first-century Christians, despite the fact that the original autographs were not still available. I Pet 1:25 --

---

[71] William F. Arndt and F. Wilbur Gingrich, A Greek-English Lexicon of the New Testament (Chicago: the University of Chicago Press, 1952), 485.

"But the word of the Lord endureth for ever. And this is the word which by the gospel is preached unto you." The eternal word was available in Peter's day. Since this is a quotation from Isa 40:8, the evidence is clear that it is proper to use this principle in a broader sense of application than just the return from captivity. Peter uses it to refer to the salvation of souls. The Word is said in v 23 to be "incorruptible," but is it found only in "corrupted" texts?

Man is frequently commanded to not revise the Word of God:

> Deut 4:2 -- Ye shall not add unto the word which I command you, neither shall ye diminish *ought* from it, that ye may keep the commandments of the LORD your God which I command you.

Deut 12:32 -- "What thing soever I command you, observe to do it: thou shalt not add thereto, nor diminish from it." Prov 30:5-6 -- "Every word of God is pure. . . . Add thou not unto his words, lest he reprove thee, and thou be found a liar."

> Rev 22:18-19 -- For I testify unto every man that heareth the words of the prophecy of this book, If any man shall add unto these things, God shall add unto him the plagues that are written in this book: And if any man shall take away from the words of the book of this prophecy, God shall take away his part out of the book of life, and out of the holy city, and from the things which are written in this book.

In these passages, judgment is pronounced upon

those who add to or take away from God's Word. Thus, the Word of God must be left untouched, for complete obedience to be possible. The emphasis is not just on "concepts," but on "words."

Bible writers pledged love and obedience to the Word of God and placed in it their hope. Without confidence in its accurate transmission to them, such hope seems misplaced: Ps 119:60-- ". . . When I have respect unto all thy commandments." Must they not be accurately known before this is assuredly possible? Ps 119:11 -- "Thy word have I hid in mine heart, that I might not sin against thee." Ps 119:16 -- ". . . I will not forget thy word." The Word must be *known* for this to be true (both then and today). Ps 119:22 -- ". . . For I have kept thy testimonies." Ps 119:42 — ". . . For I trust in thy word." Ps 119:57 -- ". . . I have said that I would keep thy words." Ps 119:69 -- ". . . But I will keep thy precepts with my whole heart." Ps 119:74 -- ". . . I have hoped in thy word." Ps 119:81, 114 -- ". . . I hope in thy word." Ps 119:93 -- "I will never forget thy precepts. . . ." Ps 119:100 -- "I understand more than the ancients, because I keep thy precepts." Ps 119:113 -- "I hate vain thoughts: but thy law do I love." The Psalmist had the confidence that he knew what were "vain thoughts" and what was God's "law," which indicates confidence in the text. Ps 119:128 -- "Therefore I esteem all thy precepts concerning all things to be right; and I hate every false way." Again, the Psalmist must have been confident that he had access to all of God's Word that had been revealed by his day, in order to know what was right and what to "hate."

> Prov 22:20-21 -- Have not I written to thee excellent things in counsels and knowledge, that I might make

thee know the certainty of the words of truth; that thou mightest answer the words of truth to them that send unto thee?

These are "words" of "certainty," not conjecture, to be used for apologetics. Lk 4:4 -- ". . . That man shall not live by bread alone, but by every word of God." Can man *live* by every word if he does not *have* every word?

One passage that has been often used by some preservationists in defense of their position is Ps 12:6-7: The words of the LORD *are* pure words: *as* silver tried in a furnace of earth, purified seven times. Thou shalt keep them, O LORD, thou shalt preserve them from this generation for ever.

In the first printing of this book, this author drew a conclusion about the passage above that needs to be corrected. While there is, in the Hebrew text, a gender discordance between "words" (feminine) in verse six and the pronoun "them" (masculine) in verse seven, it is not proper to say that it is grammatically *impossible* for the two to be referring to the same thing. In fact, Thomas Strouse, in an essay on this passage, gives examples of the same type of gender discordance used elsewhere in the Psalms in connection with God's Word (Psalm 119:11, 129, 152).[72]

---

[72] Thomas M. Strouse, "Psalm 12:6-7 and the Permanent Preservation of God's Words," essay published by Emmanuel Baptist Seminary, Newington, CT (November, 2001), 4-5.

Thus, it is certainly possible to use this passage to support the doctrine of the preservation of God's Word, although the gender discordance and the tenor of the surrounding context may allow those who disagree with the preservation concept to debate it in the passage under consideration. Because of this controversial grammatical issue, Psalm 12:6-7 may not be the best passage to use when debating with those who deny that the preservation of Scripture is taught in the Bible.

Even without Psalm 12:6-7, there is such a preponderance of Scriptures which refer to either the promise of God for preservation or the need of man for preservation that it is wise to include the preservation of the text for every generation of mankind in one's Bibliology. It deserves to be seen as Biblical fact.

Chapter 7

Historical Denial of Preservation

After the issue of the Biblical evidence for preservation of Scripture is established, the historical data must be interpreted in light of the Biblical facts. This approach is to be contrasted to that which starts with a particular interpretation of historical phenomena and adjusts doctrine to comply with that interpretation.

There is considerable reason to believe that many who have been committed to the W-H tradition of texts have demonstrated a prejudicial attitude against preservation in general, and against the TR tradition in particular:

> It is credible that very soon after its production, the fragile papyrus scroll in which Mark was written was damaged so that the last few inches were torn off, and all subsequent editions of Mark reflect this loss .[73]

After stating that the Byzantine text had been altered by copyists in the fourth century, Ladd states:

> This fact was not known in the sixteenth and seventeenth centuries when the first Greek New Testaments were printed and the King James Version translated. As we have already seen, the so-

---

[73] Ladd, 74.

> called *Textus Receptus* . . . was based on a few late minuscules, which we now know represent the latest and poorest textual family -- the Syrian or Byzantine family.[74]

> God inspired the authors of the Bible to produce a divinely superintended record, he has committed the reproduction and the preservation of the text to the vagaries of human history; and the establishment of a trustworthy text is the labor of a scientific scholarship.[75]

If these statements be accepted, then the latter portion of the Gospel of Mark has not been preserved accurately anywhere, and the local church has gone for many centuries without an accurate Bible. Since "vagaries" are whimsical, the assumption is that the preservation of God's Word is left up to chance. Such reasoning ought to cause Bible-believers to seriously question this approach.

Commenting on the promise of Biblical preservation in I Peter 1:23-25, one Fundamentalist seminary professor has said, ". . . It is speaking of the infallibility and incorruptible nature of the Word of God not of the preservation of the text of Scripture ."[76] It is dangerous for

---

[74] Ibid, 76.

[75] Ibid, 80.

[76] Glenny, 89-90.

Fundamentalists to distinguish between the "Word of God" and the "text of Scripture," since those terms are often used interchangeably.

Regarding the Greek texts used by the KJV translators, the preface to an 1881 version says:

> Their chief guides appear to have been the later editions of Stephanus and of Beza, and also, to a certain extent, the Complutensian Polyglott. All these were founded for the most part on manuscripts of late date, few in number, and used with little critical skill. But in those days it could hardly have been otherwise. Nearly all the more ancient of the documentary authorities have become known only within the last two centuries; some of the most important of them, indeed, within the last few years.[77]

Again, the question must be asked, did God *cheat* man out of the privilege of having accurate Bibles for over fourteen centuries? Is it fair to speak of the TR as "late," when the W-H text appeared in 1881?

The Westcott-Hort system of evaluating texts to determine their accuracy seems to be flawed. The following statements, taken from the Introduction to their Greek New

---

[77] Preface to The New Testament: the Old and New Versions on Opposite Pages (New York: Dodd, Mead & Company, 1881), vi.

Testament, appear to cast considerable doubt upon the method used:

> The only adequate criterion of authority for an individual document, apart from its affinity to other documents, is the character of its text, as ascertained by the fullest possible comparison of its different readings. . . . *Knowledge of documents should precede final judgement upon readings.*[78]

> The results of the interpretation of documentary evidence thus and thus alone made possible are various. In the first place, it winnows away a multitude of readings . . . (and) . . . as to supply presumptions in favour of one reading against another, varying from what amounts . . . to practically absolute certainty down to complete equipoise.[79]

"Equipoise" means evenly-balanced, or, in this case, complete inability to decide between textual variants. Also, the "multitude of readings" that are so easily "winnowed away" are the 5,250 MSS of the "family" of the TR. If that be so, how could an approach that claims to be "scientific" overlook the 5,250 MSS of the TR tradition? And how can

---

78 Westcott and Hort, 543.

79 Ibid, 546.

individual Christians make such textual judgments without access to the actual documents?

In what appears to be circular reasoning, Westcott and Hort made up their own rules for textual evaluation and then rejected the MSS which did not conform to the rules! They designed a system of evaluating Biblical texts based upon their observance and classification of genealogy, or "families" of texts. They identified "families" of texts, which they called "Western," "Alexandrian," "Neutral," and "Syrian".[80] They then proceeded to emphasize the similarities of the "Western," "Neutral," and "Alexandrian" with each other, in contrast to the "Syrian" texts. Thus, they claim that the genealogical evidence stands three-to-one in favor of their "eclectic" text! In fairness, it should have been noted that the "Syrian" group embraces approximately 93% of the discovered MSS. That does not make the "three-to-one" ratio appear quite so compelling! The Critical Text approach seems to be to establish a questionable criteria of judgment and then reject all those texts that do not meet the criteria. Following are some expressions of the W-H system: "*All trustworthy restoration of corrupted texts is founded on the study of their history, that is, of the relations of descent or affinity which connect the several documents* (emphasis his)."[81] " No available presumptions whatever as

---

[80] Ibid, 548.

[81] Ibid, 545.

to text can be obtained from number alone, that is, from number not as yet interpreted by descent."[82]

> . . . It is impossible to have any true conception of the origin of the present distribution of readings till it is clearly understood that fundamentally all textual transmission takes the form of a genealogical tree. . . . This fundamental type of transmission is indeed greatly obscured in the New Testament. . . .[83]

Unless one were already a devotee of the W-H theory, he might wonder how anything can be "clearly understood" when it is "greatly obscured!"

Although the W-H editors present their preferred MSS **B** and **Aleph** as being much older than the "Syrian" family, they acknowledge that fourth-century believers had access to the texts that followed the "Syrian" readings:

> A text virtually identical with the prevalent Greek text of the Middle Ages was used by Chrysostom and other Antiochian Fathers in the latter part of the fourth century, and thus must have been represented by MSS as old as any MS now surviving. This

---

[82] Ibid, 545.

[83] Ibid, 545-546.

> Antiochian or 'Syrian' text can frequently be recognised . . . .[84]
>
> A revision of the Old Syriac version appears to have taken place early in the fourth century, or sooner; and doubtless in some connexion with the Syrian revision of the Greek text, the readings being to a very great extent coincident.[85]

If the text was *revised* at least by early in the fourth century, its existence preceded that time. Thus, although the Syrian texts *that have been discovered* may not be as old as **B** and **Aleph**, such a text was known as far back as the time when the oldest extant ones were written. Is it fair, then, to say that **B** and **Aleph** are more reliable because they are older? Does it not seem historically probable, in light of these admissions by Westcott and Hort, that "Syrian" MSS *existed* in the earliest centuries of Church history, but have simply *not been discovered yet*? It would stand to reason that if these MSS were in popular use they would be more prone to deterioration than MSS which were distrusted and unused by believers in local churches.

Another example of the interpretation of textual history by W-H proponents is seen in this explanation in opposition to the "Byzantine" ("Syrian") text:

---

[84] Ibid, 548.

[85] Ibid, 554.

> It is also clear that the Byzantine text is a derived text. It obviously incorporates into itself the earlier readings found in both the Alexandrian and Western texts. Although the Western text is early and may be correct in some cases, it has so many additions and interpolations that few wish to defend it as a whole. A clear example of the derived nature of the Byzantine text is found in Luke 24:53 in which the disciples are described as being in the temple "praising and blessing God. . . ." The Alexandrian text has the reading "blessing God. . . ." The Western text has the reading "praising God. . . ." The Byzantine text simply put both readings together rather than omit one reading.[86]

If "older" is "better," then why does the Western text have "so many additions and interpolations?" Also, which of the two variant simple readings is to be chosen, and on what basis? When two texts differ from each other, does the critic automatically *know* which was the "chicken," and which the "egg?" Is it not possible that each of the "older" texts omitted part of that from which they copied, and could that possibility not argue that the accurate reading is found in the more complex text? If one were to extend Custer's reasoning further, would it not seem logical to accept the Gospel of Mark as authentic, based on its "simpler" version of the life of Christ, and to reject the other Gospels, which

[86] Custer, *10.*

add details not given in Mark? Although Custer, as a Fundamentalist, would never accept this logic in relation to the Gospels, such reasoning is not entirely foreign to the theological climate in which the Critical Text theory was originally produced.

However, followers of W-H do not consistently think that the simpler reading is the more likely. In fact, Nestle says just the opposite: ". . . Therefore the more difficult reading generally is acknowledged as the better one."[87] Gordon Clark evaluates this view:

> They justify this principle by assuming that the scribe is likely to think that the harder reading was a mistake, with the result that he guesses his easy interpretation is the original. No one can prove that this never happened. But it is also possible, for a number of reasons — fatigue, brilliance, the mispronunciation of a reader — that he changed an easy reading into something more difficult.[88]

Furthermore, Nestle *does* seem to endorse some kind of critical "source" theory for the Gospels when he says, "in the Gospels it is often intimated through a prefixed *p*) that

---

[87] Nestle, *67*.

[88] Gordon H. Clark, Logical Criticisms of Textual Criticism (Jefferson, Maryland: The Trinity Foundation, 1986), 16.

the reading in question has probably crept in from one of the other Gospels. . . ."[89]

The attitudes of Westcott and Hort and their followers toward the Traditional Text seem to have diverted them from truly scientific investigation of the phenomena. These attitudes can be seen in the following statements: "The number of groups that deserve serious attention is soon found to be comparatively small . . . and to a great extent they are fragmentary or discontinuous. . . ."[90]

> All the readings which have an exclusively Syrian attestation can be easily accounted for as parts of an editorial revision; and none of them have the stamp of genuineness to attest the use of extraneous and purer sources.[91]

> The Syrian text has all the appearance of being a careful attempt to supersede the chaos of rival texts by a judicious selection from them all. It would be doing violence alike to all that is known of ancient criticism . . . to imagine that the Syrian revisers would have any trustworthy means of learning

[89] Ibid, 80.

[90] Westcott and Hort, 558.

[91] Ibid, 549.

> which of the various texts, MSS, or readings had the best pedigree.[92]

"A reading marked as Syrian or Post-Syrian by the range of the documents which attest it may be safely rejected at once."[93]

It does not appear that such an off-hand rejection of the vast majority of documents is warranted by the evidence W-H gives. Should not the large group of 5250 MSS "deserve serious attention?" Is it not more "scientific" to consider *all* of the evidence seriously?

Not only did Westcott and Hort themselves express a prejudicial spirit against the TR tradition of texts, but the same is seen in some of their followers:

> It had been his (***Eberhard Nestle's***) intention to offer the result of the scientific investigation of the 19th century, instead of the still widespread cheap editions of the so-called Textus Receptus, which goes back to Erasmus. He therefore deliberately refrained from . . . subjective, critical examination of the different versions, but took as basis the great

[92] Ibid, 551.

[93] Ibid, 554.

scientific editions of the 19th century of Tischendorf (of Leipzig) and Westcott and Hort.[94]

Rather than having such a condescending attitude toward the TR, Erwin Nestle may have been wise to consider why it was so "widespread." Why would most of Church history demonstrate the preservation of a text-type that is currently denigrated as "inferior?" Was *their* knowledge inferior, or is *ours*? Eberhard Nestle's attempt to avoid subjectivity somehow allowed him to overlook the vast majority of manuscripts and take the two "scientific" editions without question! It appears that Eberhard Nestle *failed* in his attempt to avoid subjectivity.

Erwin Nestle further says:

> . . . The so-called Koine, i.e. the text-rescension which in Antioch and later in Constantinople attained general circulation (the so-called Byzantine or Imperial Text,) . . . as well as by the mass of later MSS. Since Erasmus used such late MSS for his edition, we meet this type of text in general in the Textus Receptus. . . .[95]

Why did this text, rejected by Nestle, attain "general circulation," and why does it represent the "mass of later MSS?" Is it a Biblical assumption, in light of God's

---

94 Nestle, 59.

95 Ibid, 68-69.

promises to preserve His Word for every generation, that individual Christians and local churches were deluded for centuries about the Bible? Also seemingly "unscientific" is this clear admission by Nestle: "Nevertheless of course, my father knew quite well that a certain onesidedness adhered to this text, in so far as the three collated editions rest substantially on the great Egyptian MSS. . . ."[96]

A contemptuous attitude toward the TR and the KJV was also demonstrated by the committee that produced the Revised Standard Version in the following statements: "Yet the King James Version has grave defects. . . . these defects are so many and so serious as to call for a revision of the English translation.[97] "The King James Version of the New Testament was based upon a Greek text that was marred by mistakes, containing the accumulated errors of fourteen centuries of manuscript copying."[98]

This slanted view of history is basically summarized in the attitude of Ladd:

> Since there were available to Erasmus only a half dozen late, inferior Greek manuscripts, the text which appears in the beloved Authorized or King James Version, for more than three centuries the

---

[96] Ibid, 60.

[97] Preface to Revised Standard Version, iv.

[98] Ibid, vii.

> Bible of the English-speaking world, is very inaccurate.[99]

"... The *Textus Receptus* is a poor text and is studded with thousands of textual errors, which are embodied in the beloved Authorized Version."[100]

This is an obvious rejection of preservation for every generation, if the English-speaking world had only a "very inaccurate" Bible for over 300 years! Yet, what Ladd advocates does not seem to be much of an improvement, if his own testimony is accepted:

> An evangelical criticism as well as a rationalistic criticism must often be satisfied with hypotheses, probabilities, possibilities, rather than in dogmatic certainties, as distasteful as this may be to the uncritical mind which insists on "thus saith the Lord" in every detail of Bible study.[101]

"Through the developed science of textual criticism we have achieved a relatively accurate text of the New Testament."[102]

---

[99] Ladd, 60.

[100] Ibid, 78.

[101] Ibid, 216.

[102] Ibid, 71.

For Fundamentalists, "relatively accurate" is woefully lacking! Regarding the accuracy of his brand of textual criticism, Ladd says:

> Although it can be called a science because it deals with objective facts and well-established principles, textual criticism cannot be considered a pure objective science, for at many points, as in the problem of the ending of Mark, judgments must be made, hypotheses formulated, and various possibilities debated.[103]

This sense of impreciseness seems to be characteristic of those who follow the critical approach to the text:

> Textual criticism, as applied to the Greek New Testament, forms a special study of much intricacy and difficulty, and even now leaves room for considerable variety of opinion among competent critics.[104]

> When once the ancient distribution of a reading has thus been ascertained, the characteristics of the several ancient texts furnish presumptions of the

---

[103] Ibid, 74.

[104] Preface to The New Testament: the Old and New Versions. . ., xii.

> highest value as to its genuineness or spuriousness.[105]

It would seem, then, from the statements of Westcott and Hort and some of those who follow their system, that there are some serious theological differences between the textual traditions of the TR and of W-H. Although the view of this author is that the debate should not take the form of personal attacks, there is real cause for debate, and this matter should not be taken lightly. For all those who desire to exegete God's Word in its original languages, the parsing of verbs, grammatical notations, kind and time of action, voice, mood, noun declensions, *etc.*, will be affected by the texts from which such work is done, and applications will be weakened if the text is in question.

---

105 Westcott and Hort, 554.

Chapter 8

Historical Evidence of Preservation

Although the New American Standard Version of 1963 was translated from the Critical Text, a statement in its Preface indicates the importance of the doctrine of the preservation of Scripture: "That which is forever settled in heaven (Psa.119:89) must ever be available on earth."[106] The point of this study is to show that it *has* been available on earth throughout Church history in the Traditional Text. John Burgon provides this explanation:

> . . . The Texts of Erasmus (1516) and of Stunica (1522). . . . derived from independent sources . . . exhibits (*under the good Providence of God,*) a Traditional Text, the general purity of which is demonstrated by all the evidence which 350 years of subsequent research have succeeded in accumulating; and which is confessedly the Text of A.D. 375.[107]
>
> Call this text Erasmian or Complutensian, -- the Text of Stephens, or of Beza, or of the Elzevirs, -- call it the 'Received,' or the *Traditional Greek Text*,

---

[106] Preface to The Dynamite of God: New American Standard Bible New Testament (New York: New York Bible Society, 1963), vi.

[107] John William Burgon, The Revision Revised, 1883, (Collingswood, NJ: reprinted by The Bible for Today), 250.

> or whatever other name you please; -- the fact remains, that a Text *has* come down to us which is attested by a general consensus of ancient Copies, ancient Fathers, ancient Versions. This, at all events, is a point on which, (happily,) there exists entire conformity of opinion between Dr. Hort and ourselves.[108]

A recent challenge has been made to the TR on the basis of the limited number of MSS that Erasmus used in producing his version of the text. At the risk of redundancy, one opponent made these statements:

> . . . The *Textus Receptus* . . . which only represents about a half dozen manuscripts of the Byzantine text-type. . . . Consequently, in eight months Erasmus edited his Greek NT based on the seven manuscripts available to him at Basel. . . . Of the seven manuscripts which Erasmus used, none contained the whole NT. . . . As a result of his editing of these seven manuscripts, in 1516 Erasmus produced a new Greek text which had never existed before. . . . the TR is only based on seven late manuscripts. . . . However we believe the best Greek texts available consider all the manuscripts . . . and

[108] Ibid, 269.

especially not only the seven that were used by Erasmus when he edited the TR.[109]

The roots of the TR are found to be very early in Christian history! Both W-H and Burgon conclude that the TR is not significantly changed from its Syrian and Byzantine predecessors, so perhaps the above emphasis is unfair, especially in light of the adoption of a minority of available texts by W-H. Burgon, however, anticipated this criticism of Erasmus:

> If the objection be made, as it probably will be, "Do you then mean to rest upon the five manuscripts used by Erasmus?" I reply, that the copies employed were selected because they were known to represent with accuracy the Sacred Word; that the descent of the text was evidently guarded with jealous care . . . that it rests mainly upon much the widest testimony . . . .[110]

It appears to this author that the opponents of Erasmus and the TR textual tradition are criticizing Erasmus for doing what they themselves are doing. . . textual criticism. How odd that they would make such an issue of the small *number* of MSS used by that editor when they

---

[109] Glenny, 47-51, 130.

[110] John William Burgon, The Traditional Text, 1896, (Collingswood, NJ: reprinted by The Bible for Today), 15.

follow a position that espouses the *minority* of extant MSS as superior today! Had Erasmus' few MSS disagreed with that which local churches were using, there would be reason to reject his work, but if he purposely chose the texts that best represent the churches' tradition, the results seem legitimate.

Church history has left a trail of evidence of the New Testament texts used by both the orthodox and the heretical. The writings of the Church Fathers are actually the oldest documents that have been discovered, and their Scripture quotations and references to available texts show their textual preferences. The Church Fathers were simply early professing Christians whose writings have been discovered. They are usually divided according to their approximate relationship in time to the Council of Nicea, which took place in 325 AD. Those who lived prior to that Council are called "Ante-Nicene," and those who came later are designated "Post-Nicene." The Versions, or ancient translations of the Greek into other languages, date as far back as the second century, and appear to reveal textual preferences. The Uncials were the oldest Greek MSS discovered, dating back to the third or fourth century. They were written as continuous capital letters, without spaces between words or sentences. They are sometimes referred to as "majuscules." The Cursives were Greek MSS dating from the eighth century onward. They utilize small letters as well as spaces between the words, and have been called "miniscules." Many miniscules have been found, and they overwhelmingly endorse the TR tradition of text. The Lectionaries were used in public worship services, including Scripture readings along with "pulpit" comments, which give indications of the texts used. The oldest Lectionaries found date from the eighth century, but statements from the church fathers seem to indicate that they were in existence much earlier.

The Church Fathers have shown a preference for the Traditional Text, according to the research of Burgon and his associate, Edward Miller. Miller's approach seems to be thorough:

> Accordingly, I made a toilsome examination for myself of the Fathers before St. Chrysostom, or as I defined them in order to draw a self-acting line, of those who died before 400 A.D., with the result that the Traditional Text is found to stand in the general proportion of 3:2 against other variations, and in a much higher proportion upon thirty test passages. Afterwards, not being satisfied with resting the basis of my argument upon one scrutiny, I went again through the writings of the seventy-six Fathers concerned, . . . besides others who yielded no evidence, and I found that although several more instances were consequently entered in my note-book, the general results remained almost the same. . . . I claim, not only that my attempts have been honest and fair even to self-abnegation, but that the general results which are much more than is

> required by my argument . . . abundantly establish the antiquity of the Traditional Text, by proving the superior acceptance of it during the period at stake to that of any other. Indeed, these examinations have seemed to me . . . to carry back the Traditional Text satisfactorily to the first age. . . .[111]

> The sole duty of the Textual Critic is found in assembling, weighing, and balancing the different kinds of evidence that can be brought to bear upon the passage under review. There is no demand therefore for conjecture; it is an ascertainment of facts: besides that conjecture or surmise are entirely excluded by reason of the peculiar dignity and loftiness of the subject.[112]

This appears to strikingly contrast with Westcott and Hort's admitted "conjectures." Apparently the Critical approach did not follow the meticulousness demonstrated by Miller:

> And Hort's theory, as will be shewn (*sic*) further on, involves too much violation of principles generally received, and is too devoid of anything like proof,

---

[111] Edward Miller in the Preface to John William Burgon, The Traditional Text, x.

[112] Edward Miller, A Guide to the Textual Criticism of the New Testament, 1886, (Collingswood, NJ: reprinted by the Dean Burgon Society, Inc.), 65-66.

> ever to win universal acceptance. As matters of fact easily verified, it stands in sharp antagonism to the judgement passed by the Church all down the ages, and in many respects does not accord with the teaching of the most celebrated critics of the century who preceded him.[113]

Miller notes that heresy invaded Christianity very early in its history, resulting in tampering with the text:

> But Basilides, who lived in the earlier half of the second century, a native of Alexandria, the chief seat and centre (*sic*) of Gnosticism, rejected the Pastoral Epistles and the Epistle to the Hebrews, and added other books to those which were canonically recognized. After him Valentinus is said by Tertullian to have corrected the text and to have boldly maintained that readings introduced by him were older than the words generally received. Marcion went much further . . . . According to Tertullian and Epiphanius, he "mutilated and depraved" the text both of Epistles and Gospels. Nor must Tatian be omitted, a disciple of Justin Martyr, and founder of the Sect of the Encratites. . . . Thus Dionysius of Corinth says that he must not be surprised when people altered his writings by additions and omissions, if they tampered in like

---

[113] Burgon, The Traditional Text, 7.

> manner with the Holy Scriptures. St. Irenaeus tells the same story, and appears to have had the same fear. Clement of Alexandria complains of people who introduce change into the Gospels. An unknown writer, quoted by Eusebius, inveighs against heretics who laid hands without fear upon the Divine Scriptures, under the pretence (*sic*) of correcting them.[114]

Miller then asserts that his research pointed to the fact of textual preservation:

> And yet indications are not wanting that exceeding care was taken by the orthodox to preserve the Holy Books in their genuine and unimpaired form. Tertullian, in arguing with heretics, bids them consult the autographs of the Apostles at Corinth, or Thessalonica, or Ephesus, or Rome, where they are preserved and read in public. St. Irenaeus refers in one place to 'the approved and ancient copies' for settling the number 666 in the Revelation; and in another gives most particular directions as to the careful and correct copying of a book of his own.[115]

---

[114] Miller, A Guide . . ., 70-72.

[115] Ibid, 72.

The Traditional Text is seen by Miller to have appeared in the writings of the Ante-Nicene Fathers (those who died prior to 400 AD):

> We are, however, not left to secondary evidence for proof that the Traditional Text was used and handed on in Ante-Nicene days. The witness of separate ecclesiastical writers upon controverted passages, proving that they had in their possession manuscripts agreeing with the Text afterwards adopted generally in the Church, and the renderings of the early Versions, especially the Syriac and Italic, establish satisfactorily this position. . . .[116]
>
> After listing 38 specific examples, Miller says:
>
> That is to say, in 165 places as relating to only 15 chance passages in Holy Scripture Ecclesiastical Writers living before the Era of St. Chrysostom are proved to have followed Manuscripts thus witnessing to the Traditional Text. It should be born in mind that it was only at the close of this period that ***Aleph*** and **B**, the two oldest manuscripts now existing, were produced.[117]
>
> In a similar manner, the Peshito and Italic Versions -- including under the latter class the best of the Old

---

[116] Ibid, 73.

[117] Ibid, 85.

Latin Versions -- were made two hundred years before those two Manuscripts (***Aleph*** and **B**), and -- especially the former -- support the Traditional Text. . . . There is therefore, as these specimens show, no warrant for asserting that the Traditional Text is not traceable back as far as the earliest age of the Church.[118]

The Peshito, or "Simple" Version has remained certainly since the sad divisions wrought in the Syrian Church during the fifth century, because the Nestorians and Monophysites, as well as the Christians of St. Thomas in India and the Maronites of Lebanon, all use it to this day, and prove therefore by such use that we must go back for its origin at least to the time when they had not separated. And it appears most probable, that it was that which was read at the first in Syria. Hegesippus, in the second century, seems to speak of a Syrian translation, and Melito quotes "the Syrian" in 170 A.D. Ephraem of Edessa speaks of this Version as used familiarly for the national Scriptures in the fourth century. The Peshito resembles the Received Text.[119]

---

[118] Ibid, 85.

[119] Ibid, 74-75.

A modern writer gives evidence of the antiquity of the Traditional (Byzantine) text with the following notation:

> Sturz documents the existence in recently discovered papyri of hundreds of variant readings previously identified as distinctly Byzantine. . . . These readings show up centuries before the bulk of the Byzantine family manuscripts, and suggest that many readings of the distinctly "Byzantine" text type were established in the second century rather than the fourth, or later, as is conjectured by opponents of the Byzantine text type.[120]

Miller voices his assessment of the likely value of the Syrian Greek texts over the Western:

> Whilst in Syria Greek was well understood, and it must have been easy there to get at the autographs themselves, or at excellent copies made directly from the autographs, in Italy, Africa, and in the other parts of the West, accurate acquaintance with Greek was comparatively rare, and the distance must have led to a large crop of mistakes.[121]

After listing five ancient libraries that contained a total of over 600,000 volumes available to the Post-

---

[120] William Smallman, in From the Mind of God to the Mind of Man, 179.

[121] Ibid, 76.

Nicene Fathers, Miller gives credence to their strongly-united voice regarding the Traditional Text:

> It seems surely clear from these considerations that we of the present time are so inferior to the Churchmen of the age of St. Chrysostom and of the succeeding ages, both in the furniture of our "apparatus criticus" and in the knowledge of early manuscripts, that it would be rash in the extreme to overrule the verdict which they passed. And this conclusion is surely strengthened almost to demonstration, when we take into consideration the overruling care of the Holy Ghost in the Church. For the Church does not act by Councils alone, or solely in Canons or Creeds, but expresses her decisions in the universal operations of her common life.[122]

> Various indications, occurring as if by chance here and there amidst discussions, prove that the learned men of this period were quite alive to the variations of manuscripts, and exercised critical judgment in deciding between conflicting readings.[123]

Perhaps without realizing the historical implications of the admission, a W-H proponent stated:

---

[122] Ibid, 91.

[123] Ibid, 96.

> Many of the Greek manuscripts contain a text of the New Testament which was standardized in the fifth century AD. The first printed edition of the Greek text came in 1516 -- in a form prepared by the Dutch scholar Erasmus. Up until then no-one had questioned the accuracy of this text.[124]

This statement about the Universal acceptance of the TR tradition for over one thousand years is made despite the writer's commitment to modern textual criticism, which he explains in his following two paragraphs. If the doctrine of preservation for every generation be accepted, the above argument attests the validity of the TR, not the Critical Text.

The following chart explains the various sources of textual evidence in the earliest centuries of church history. It describes the chief forms in which textual information has come to archaeologists, who have attempted to discern which textual traditions were available and used by believers early in the history of local churches. These include the writings of the church fathers, with Scripture quotations that give evidence of their textual preferences, as well as the ancient versions, uncial and cursive manuscripts, and the lectionaries, which also contained quotations from Scripture.

---

[124] Pat Alexander, ed., The Lion Encyclopedia Bible, Lion Publishing Corporation, (reprinted by the Reader's Digest Association, Inc., 1987), 70.

Ancient Documents and the Text

Writings of the Church Fathers

1. The oldest writings found.
2. Quotations and references to available texts.

Versions

1. Translations of texts into different languages.
2. Oldest found date back to the 2nd century.

Uncials

1. Oldest MSS discovered, 3rd or 4th century.
2. Capital letters, without spaces.

Cursives

1. Date from the 8th century and later.
2. Many have been found.
3. Vastly support the TR tradition of text.

Lectionaries

1. Used in public worship services.
2. Found from 8th century and later.
3. Church Fathers seem to have had them.

Burgon further attacks the system of Westcott and Hort with specific indictments:

> So far from thinking with Dr. Hort that "the value of the evidence obtained from Transcriptional Probability is incontestable," -- for that, "without its aid, Textual Criticism could rarely obtain a high degree of security," (p. 24) -- we venture to declare that inasmuch as one expert's notions of what is "transcriptionally probable" prove to be the diametrical reverse of another expert's notions, the supposed evidence to be derived from this source may, with advantage, be neglected altogether. Let the study of *Documentary Evidence* be allowed to take its place. Notions of "Probability" are the very pest of those departments of Science which admit of an appeal to *Fact*.[125]
>
> Dr. Hort is for setting up what his own inner consciousness "pronounces to be right," against "Documentary Evidence," however multitudinous. He claims that his own verifying faculty shall be supreme, -- shall settle every question.[126]
>
> . . . We are disposed to maintain that "a majority of extant documents" in the proportion of 995 to 5, --

---

[125] Burgon, The Revision Revised, 252.

[126] Ibid, 253.

and sometimes of 1999 to 1, -- creates more than "a presumption." It amounts to *Proof of a majority of ancestral documents.*[127]

But then, it happens, unfortunately, that we are unacquainted with *one single instance* of a known MS. copied from another known MS. And perforce all talk about "Genealogical evidence," where *no single step in the descent* can be produced, -- in other words, *where no Genealogical evidence exists*, -- is absurd.[128]

. . . Will any Reader of ordinary fairness and intelligence be surprised to hear that we reject the assumed "Conflation" unconditionally, as a silly dream? It is founded entirely upon the omission of 21 (or at most 42) words out of a total of 31,587 from Codd. **B *Aleph* D**. And yet it is demonstrable that out of that total, **B** omits 1519: ***Aleph***, 1686: **D**, 2452.[129]

It becomes apparent that we have to do with a Writer who has discovered a summary way of dealing with the Text of Scripure, and who is

---

[127] Ibid, 255.

[128] Ibid, 256.

[129] Ibid, 264-265.

> prepared to impart his secret to any who care to accept -- without questioning -- his views.[130]
>
> The natural and even necessary correlative of this, has been the disparagement of the merits of the commonly Received Text: which has come to be spoken of (we know not why), as contemptuously, almost as bitterly, as if it had been at last ascertained to be untrustworthy in every respect: a thing undeserving alike of a place and of a name among the monuments of the Past.[131]

Burgon's seven "Tests of Truth," which are actually his principles of textual criticism, are as follows:

> 1. Antiquity, or Primitiveness; 2. Consent of Witnesses, or Number; 3. Variety of Evidence, or Catholicity; 4. Respectability of Witnesses, or Weight; 5. Continuity, or Unbroken Tradition; 6. Evidence of the Entire Passage, or Context; 7. Internal Considerations, or Reasonableness.[132]

Using this system, Burgon drew the conclusions that form the basis for this study:

---

[130] Ibid, 268.

[131] Ibid, 270.

[132] Burgon, The Traditional Text, 29.

Let it then be remembered, that a wealth of copies existed in early times; that the need of zealous care of the Holy Scriptures was always felt in the Church; that it is only from the Church that we have learnt which are the books of the Bible and which are not; that in the age in which the Canon was settled, and which is presumed by many critics to have introduced a corrupted text, most of the intellect of the Roman Empire was found within the Church, and was directed upon disputed questions; that in the succeeding ages the art of transcribing was brought to a high pitch of perfection; and that the verdict of all the several periods since the production of those two manuscripts has been given till a few years ago in favour of the Text which has been handed down: -- let it be further borne in mind that the testimony is not only that of all the ages, but of all the countries: and at the very least so strong a presumption will ensue on behalf of the Traditional Text, that a powerful case indeed must be constructed to upset it.[133]

One and the same Traditional Text, except in comparatively few particulars, has prevailed in the Church from the beginning till now. Especially deserving of attention is the admission that the Text in question is of the fourth century, to which same

---

[133] Ibid, 12-13.

> century the two oldest of our Sacred Codexes (B and Aleph) belong. There is observed to exist in Church Lectionaries precisely the same phenomenon.[134]
>
> . . . The whole of the controversy may be reduced to the following narrow issue: Does the truth of the Text of Scripture dwell with the vast multitude of copies, uncial and cursive, concerning which nothing is more remarkable than the marvellous (*sic*) agreement which subsists between them? Or is it rather to be supposed that the truth abides exclusively with a very little handful of manuscripts, which at once differ from the great bulk of the witnesses, and -- strange to say -- also amongst themselves?[135]

A summary of Burgon's conclusions, explaining his interpretation of the historical evidence should be carefully considered:

> That a perpetual miracle was wrought for their preservation -- that copyists were protected against the risk of error, or evil men prevented from adulterating shamefully copies of the Deposit -- no one, it is presumed, is so weak as to suppose. But it is quite a different thing to claim that all down the

---

134 Ibid, 14-15.

135 Ibid, 16-17.

ages the sacred writings must needs have been God's peculiar care; that the Church under Him has watched over them with intelligence and skill; has recognized which copies exhibit a fabricated, which an honestly transcribed text; has generally sanctioned the one, and generally disallowed the other. I am utterly disinclined to believe -- so grossly improbable does it seem -- that at the end of 1800 years 995 copies out of every thousand, suppose, will prove untrustworthy; and that the one, two, three, four or five which remain, whose contents were till yesterday as good as unknown, will be found to have retained the secret of what the Holy Spirit originally inspired. I am utterly unable to believe, in short, that God's promise has so entirely failed, that at the end of 1800 years much of the text of the Gospel had in point of fact to be picked by a German critic out of a waste-paper basket in the convent of St. Catherine; and that the entire text had to be remodelled (*sic*) after the pattern set by a couple of copies which had remained in neglect during fifteen centuries, and had probably owed their survival to that neglect; whilst hundreds of others had been thumbed to pieces, and had bequeathed their witness to copies made from them.[136]

---

[136] Ibid, 11-12.

A final word of exhortation comes from the defender of the Traditional Text:

> Beyond all things I claim at every thoughtful reader's hands that he will endeavor to approach this subject in an impartial frame of mind. To expect that he will succeed in divesting himself of all preconceived notions as to what is likely, what not, were unreasonable. But he is invited at least to wear his prejudices as loose about him as he can; to be prepared to cast them off if at any time he has been shewn (*sic*) that they are founded on misapprehension; to resolve on taking nothing for granted which admits of being proved to be either true or false.[137]

The chart below is a brief view of the eras of Church history when certain MSS and versions appeared and prevailed. Although no Traditional-type MSS have been discovered that demonstrably can be dated from the first four centuries, the Peshitta was a second-century Syriac version that pointed to the prior existence of the TR tradition. Ante-Nicene references to a "Syrian" text validate this conclusion. The chart also demonstrates the great dominance of the Traditional-type text in the Post-Nicene era, down through the Middle Ages, and on through the Reformation period. While the chart is admittedly

---

[137] Ibid, 8.

sketchy in details, it is fairly representative of the historical sequence of events regarding the availability of the text-types.

History of Textual Transmission

W-H Text	Date (AD)	TR Tradition
	200	Peshitta
Sinaiticus/Vaticanus	400	
	500	Cd Alexandrinus
	600	Cd Basiliensis
Very few copies	700-900	Many copies
	1000	1,997 copies
	1500	Erasmus, Stephanus
	1600	Beza, Elzivirs
W-H, ASV	1900	
RSV NASV NIV TEV	2000	NKJV
Approximately 400 MSS found		Approximately 5200 MSS found

Chapter 9

The Vehicle of Preservation

It has been asserted here that God promised to preserve the text of His Word, and that Biblical evidence of such preservation can be seen in the New Testament. Of particular interest is the indication in II Timothy 3:15-16 that the "God-breathed" Scriptures were known to Timothy centuries after the writing of the originals. If it be accepted that God made a preservation promise, and that He kept the promise at least through the New Testament era, the next step is to see how God kept that promise in Post-Apostolic times. There seems to be Bible evidence to conclude that God intended for the local church to be the primary vehicle through which He would preserve His Word. One passage to be considered is Jude 3:

> Beloved, when I gave all diligence to write unto you of the common salvation, it was needful for me to write unto you, and exhort *you* that ye should earnestly contend for the faith which was once delivered unto the saints.

Jude's Epistle, which is a companion to II Peter, warns about creeping apostasy and challenges believers in the local church to guard against it. In this struggle, believers are to depend upon the God who is "able to keep you from falling (v 24)." Thus, the God who preserves believers is about to commission believers to be active in the preservation of His Word.

The Greek word translated "contend" is from *epagonizomai*, which is summarized by the Theological Dictionary of the New Testament as encompassing the ideas of full exertion, rigid discipline, facing opposition (perhaps even martyrdom), and the responsibility that believers have to help others.[138] As a present-tense infinitive, the challenge then is to continuation, despite hardships, for the benefit of others. The term "faith" is *pistis*, which signifies, in this instance, ". . . the orthodox doctrine handed down by the church. . . ."[139] "Once" is *hapax*, used of the death of Christ (Heb 9:26-28; I Pet 3:18) and of man (Heb 9:27). The sense of this word is "once for all," indicating "something which cannot be repeated."[140] "Delivered" is an aorist passive participle, which speaks of something that has taken place at some point in the past. It signifies being "handed over," as in a trial or betrayal, and when used of teachings (as in Jude 3) it has the connotation of oral traditions.

---

[138] Gerhard Kittel, editor, Theological Dictionary of the New Testament (Grand Rapids: Wm. B. Eerdmans Publishing Company, 1991), I, 137-138.

[139] Ibid., VI, 213.

[140] Ibid., I, 381-383.

Thus, a specific body of doctrines has been "handed over" to the saints, for protection and control, and it is so precise as to warrant "contending" for its details. It has specifically been "handed over" to *saints*, as opposed to the unbelieving world, and the saints are to see the reception of Scripture as a "once for all" experience. Believers are to practice rigid discipline in the process, facing great obstacles, with the spiritual needs of others as part of their motivation for exertion. It seems, then, that the God who preserves His saints also intended to preserve His word through the vigilance of His saints, and that such preservation would benefit generations of mankind that were yet future when Jude wrote. Thus, it is both Biblical and logical to look to the saints of church history for their testimony regarding the text of Scripture.

As stated, II Peter is a companion book to the Epistle of Jude. There Peter also warns about false prophets and teachers whose influence would result in apostate doctrine and living. In an often-cited passage about the *inspiration* of Scriptures, II Peter 1:21, there is a contextual indication of the *preservation* of Scriptures. Verse nineteen says, "We have also a more sure word of prophecy (referring to the Word of God) . . . ." With this statement, Peter is asserting that the words which were spoken by "holy men of God" were still in his possession centuries after their original writing. Peter's audience also had access to these words, for they are challenged to "take heed" to them in verse twenty.

The same theme is followed by Peter in the third chapter of this epistle. In verse two he admonishes his readers to be ". . . mindful of the words which were spoken before by the holy prophets . . . ." His emphasis is upon *words*, not just *concepts*. With reference to the exegesis of II Peter 3:1-3 and the usage of *mimneskesthai* ("mindful"), the Theological Dictionary of the New Testament says:

> (*Mimneskesthai*) . . . is not meant in a historicising or intellectualistic sense in the NT, though it easily misunderstood (*sic*) along these lines. What is at issue is neither the quickening of a past tradition nor the keeping in memory of religious truths, but a specific understanding of the Word of God as this emerges especially at a later time.[141]

The usage of *rhematon* ("words"), particularly since it is plural, focuses beyond mere concepts or ideas to the actual *words* used to express those ideas. Peter's message, then, has the connotation that "at a later time" it will be extremely important to have the very *words* spoken by the prophets, the apostles, and the Savior.

Peter concludes his second epistle by noting man's tendency to "wrest," or pervert, the Scriptures (3:16), challenging believers to beware of being led into error and falling from steadfastness (verse seventeen). It stands to reason that this challenge would include the need to be

---

[141] Ibid., IV, 678.

vigilant over the words of the text as the principal protection from error.

Another quite significant passage in this regard is I Timothy 3:15. Appearing in one of the Pastoral epistles, this has immediate application to the local church. Chapter three gives qualifications for the offices of pastor and deacon, then explains why this instruction is given:

> But if I tarry long, that thou mayest know how thou oughtest to behave thyself in the house of God, which is the church of the living God, the pillar and ground of the truth.

Since the local church is seen to be the "pillar and ground of the truth," these terms deserve further analysis. "Pillar" is from *stulos*, which was literally a "support or carrier."[142] It is used metaphorically in Galatians 2:9 to refer to spiritual leaders as "pillars." This same metaphorical use appears in I Timothy 3:15, with the exception that the "pillar" is the local church itself, not just a few leaders. The indication is that the local church supports and carries God's truth. Thayer says that *stulos* " . . . is used of persons to whose eminence and strength the stability and authority of any institution or organization are due . . . ."[143] In this

---

[142] Ibid., VII, 733.

[143] Joseph Henry Thayer, ed., A Greek-English Lexicon of the New Testament, (Edinburgh: T. & T. Clark, 1955), 591.

passage, then, the local church would provide that eminence and strength, ensuring the stability and authority of the truth. Of course, the church is not the *source* of that stability, but is merely the *instrument* of it. The word translated "ground" is *hedraioma*, of which Kittel says:

> A Church is established which protects and defends the truth against the confusion of myths. . . . It gives the faith and thinking of individuals a sure ground in confession (cf 3:16 etc.) No longer God alone, but also the Church of God, now guarantees the permanence of the (*alethia*).[144]

The teaching of this passage seems to be that God gave to the church the responsibility to support, carry, protect, and maintain the accuracy and the authority of the truth. The church, then, becomes the instrument of God's preservation of His Word. Thus, the truth should be found in the possession of local churches throughout this Dispensation. This argues against the theory that the Scriptures were lost to the general public for centuries.

There are also numerous charges in the New Testament epistles regarding the special care that pastors and other believers should take with the Word of God and its doctrines. Good pastors are characterized as those who "labour in the word and doctrine (I Tim 5:17)." One of the qualifications for the office of pastor is "holding fast the

---

[144] Kittel, II, 364.

faithful word . . . (Titus 1:9)." Deacons were to be "Holding the mystery of the faith in a pure conscience (I Tim 3:9)." Paul told Timothy, "Take heed unto thyself and unto the doctrine; continue in them. . . .(I Tim 4:16);" "But continue thou in the things which thou hast learned. . . .(II Tim 3:14);" "That thou keep *this* commandment without spot. . . .(I Tim 6:14);" " . . . Keep that which is committed to thy trust. . . . (I Tim 6:20);" "Hold fast the form of sound words. . . . (II Tim 1:13);" and "That good thing which was committed unto thee keep by the Holy Ghost. . . . (II Tim 1:14)." The Corinthians were instructed to " . . . keep the ordinances, as I delivered *them* to you (I Cor 11:2)." Paul desired for the Philippian believers to be found, "Holding forth the word of life. . . . (Phil 2:16)."

These and other passages give weighty responsibility to the local church and its leaders for precise remembrance, obedience, and propagation with regard to the doctrines of the Word of God. These doctrines, of course, are preserved in *words*. The most accurate way to preserve the doctrines is to preserve the *words* in which they were expressed. This was clearly illustrated early in Church history, when the conflict at the Council of Nicea between Athanasius and Arius over the nature of Christ revolved around the inclusion or exclusion of one Greek letter (*iota*) in the doctrinal statement. Athanasius demanded that the statement say that Christ was *identical* in essence (*homoousios*) with the Father, while Arius would only agree that Christ was *similar* in essence (*homoiousios*). Thus, the addition of one Greek letter undermined the doctrine of the Deity of Christ. Thankfully, Athanasius' position prevailed at Nicea.[145] However, it seems a fair conclusion that if one Greek letter could so significantly change the meaning of a doctrinal statement, changes in the wording of the Biblical text could also have a dramatic impact upon doctrine and practice.

The passages viewed in this section point to the fact that the first-century churches and their leaders were commissioned to vigilantly guard the text of the Scriptures. Careful attention to *every word* is the only way that all of the above commands could have been obeyed. It must also be noted that these commandments leave an implied challenge to all local churches and church leaders who have since existed to accept the same responsibility.

There is a very real sense in which all Bible-believers, regardless of their textual preferences, have acknowledged the role that local churches and their leaders have played in the preservation of the Bible. Historians have credited early believers with the *canonization* of the Scriptures, which is not to say that they established a new Bible, but that they merely acknowledged what they had always accepted to be Scripture. Canonization should be seen as one step taken toward the fulfillment of Paul's

---

[145] Albert Henry Newman, A Manual of Church History (Chicago: The American Baptist Publication Society, 1957), I, 330.

charge for *preservation* of the Scripture. Canonization was the statement of the Post-Apostolic churches regarding the preservation of the sixty-six books that Fundamentalists still accept as God's Word. Those who accept the churches' pronouncement in *canonization* should also accept their pronouncement in *preservation*, for in fact, canonization *is* preservation. The theological justification for canonization is also justification for the doctrine of the preservation of Scripture. The *books* that churches approved as authoritative were comprised of *words*. It seems highly illogical to look to the local churches of history for their stamp of approval upon *books* of Scripture and then reject the *words* found in those books. Summarizing a discussion about canonization, one writer has stated:

> Having settled the primary issue of which *books* were to be recognized as Scripture, a secondary level of evaluation was needed to determine which *copies* of those books best represented the exact text of the original. The history of that evaluation goes beyond the scope of a discussion of the issues of canonicity but should be understood as a proper and necessary extension of the same process.[146]

For a pure text, then, one should look to that text which local churches and church leaders throughout their

---

[146] Paul W. Downey, in From the Mind of God ..., 62.

history have used. That text has been, without question, the tradition that produced the *Textus Receptus*.

Chapter 10

What About Translations?

But what of the English translation controversy? Peter Ruckman has been quoted as saying, "The A.V. 1611 is necessary to recover the original text and straighten out the corrupt Greek."[147] If Ruckman were right, then for centuries before 1611 men did not have the preserved Word of God. This view may allow for the preservation of Scripture *since* 1611, but seems to be woefully lacking about the preservation of Scripture *before* 1611.

The view advocated here is that God has promised to preserve His Word, and it is preserved for the English-speaking world in the KJV, but it has also been preserved by God for non-English-speaking people in good translations of the Greek TR and the Hebrew Masoretic Text into other languages. Since none of these translations existed when the original texts were written, and God did not promise to extend inspiration to the then-future translations, there can be no *Biblical proof* for the inspiration of translations. All that the Bible addresses as being inspired ("God-breathed") are the original autographs. Inspiration and new revelation ceased with the completion of the Book of Revelation in 96 AD. Without a promise from God to inspire a future translation and without His identification of *which* translation that might be, one should not accept the extra-

---

[147] Custer, Does Inspiration . . ., 21, quoting Peter Ruckman, The Christian's Handbook of Manuscript Evidence, 120.

Biblical position of the inspiration of translations. If the Apostle Paul had written that in 1611 God would give a new English translation for the world to heed, Fundamentalism's position would be different. It must be remembered that what the KJV says about the exclusivity of *its* text, the NIV also says about *its* text. If one assumes that God "breathed" again in 1611, he opens the door for the Charismatics and others who claim to be getting new revelations from God today. This position is clearly in theological error. In summary, since God did not *promise* to inspire future translations, there is no *Biblical* basis to believe in their inspiration, and the issue of translations should not become a test of fellowship.

It may be helpful, nevertheless, to briefly address the issue of translations. There are two important ways to evaluate translations. The first consideration is the main issue of this book, namely, which original language texts are used. A good translation of flawed texts will be automatically flawed. The second consideration is the particular translation philosophy adopted by the translators. The two principle philosophies are termed *formal equivalency* and *dynamic equivalency*. Formal equivalency attempts to translate what the text actually *says* in the original. It is called "formal" because it follows the same *form* as the original, where possible. Dynamic equivalency, on the other hand, describes what the translators think it *means*. It is considered "dynamic" because it gives latitude to change the wording in order to convey the perceived sense. This, then, may occasionally tend to be more an editorial commentary than a translation. The KJV is a formal equivalency translation of the TR; the New American Standard Version (NASV) is a formal equivalency translation of the Critical Text; and the New International Version (NIV) and Today's English Version (TEV) are dynamic equivalency translations of the Critical Text. While none of these deserves to be called "heretical," both the choice of original texts and the translation philosophy will have bearing upon their accuracy. For proponents of the CT, the NASV should be seen as a superior translation, because its translation philosophy makes it a more accurate rendering of the original than are the NIV and TEV. However, those who choose the TR over the CT should prefer the KJV above the NASV, because while they may both be excellent translations, the KJV is a translation of a *text* that is considered superior. Furthermore, since virtually all of the modern translations are renditions of the CT with varying degrees of accuracy, the KJV is considered here to be superior to all of them.

The distinctions between translations can be seen in many places, but perhaps Matthew 6:33 can serve as an illustration. The KJV says, "But seek ye first the kingdom of God, and his righteousness; and all these things shall be added unto you." This is a good formal equivalency of the TR. Since the CT omits the Greek word *Theos*, the name of God does not appear in those versions translated from it. The NASV says, "But seek first His kingdom, and His righteousness, and all these things shall be added to you." This represents formal equivalency of the CT. Slightly more liberty is taken by the NIV to produce, "But seek first his kingdom and his righteousness, and all these things will be given to you as well." The particular edition consulted (second edition, eighth printing) did not use italics to identify their addition of "as well," even though that addition is not justified by the Greek text used. Also, there is not a grammatical reason to change "added" to "given." A still further attempt to be "dynamic" is seen in the TEV: "Instead, give first place to his Kingdom and to what he requires, and he will provide you with all these other things." In this rendition, "seek first" is changed to "give first place," "righteousness" is replaced with "what he requires," "added" becomes "provided," and the word "other" is included, all without textual justification. The TEV, then, becomes more like a commentary than a translation. The translators are evidently giving their readers what they think the passage *means*, rather than what it actually *says*. Hopefully, this comparison will show the importance of having not only the best *Greek text*, but also the proper *translation philosophy*. It is asserted here that the KJV satisfies both criteria for judgment.

Chapter 11

Some Practical Considerations

Why is it so important that the very *words* of Scripture be preserved for use today? Obviously, the most significant reason is the protection of the integrity of the God Who promised to preserve it. However, there are many practical issues that are affected if churches and individual believers today do not have access to God's precise Word.

An individual believer might question his own obedience to God as he prepares to give account at the Judgment Seat of Christ. How would one *know* whether he had been obedient if the *words* that he must obey were in doubt?

If the precision of God's Word is in doubt, then so will be its authority. The question of the day will be that of Satan in Genesis 3:1: "Yea, hath God said? . . ." When a witnessing Christian claims, "The Bible says, . . ." the confused unbeliever might ask, "Which Bible?" There has already been enough controversy over the textual issue to give God's enemies cause to mock.

When a preacher stands in his pulpit and proclaims, "Thus saith the LORD . . . ," his words might seem empty and fall on deaf ears if the text is in doubt. Could not such a situation give a plausible excuse to those who ". . . shall turn away *their* ears from the truth, and be turned unto fables (II Tim 4:4)?"

One who follows the Critical Text method suggests the following system of studying the New Testament:

> Therefore, the only honest alternative left for us is to study all the manuscripts available to us for the purpose of compiling a text better than the best found in any one manuscript or group of manuscripts.[148]

But who has done this? Since the extant MSS are located in various countries of the world and primarily appear as museum artifacts, must one travel the world and compare 5,656 documents every time he chooses to translate a verse from the Greek New Testament? Does any professor, preacher, or student actually follow such a procedure? By this criterion, how many Bible students could be considered "honest?" How many Fundamentalist Bible colleges and seminaries are "honest" in their Greek classrooms?

Even if one were to do such a search, is it not possible that he might come up with a different "preserved" Word than another individual might in his search? Without a commonly-accepted text, are not believers left with mere "concept preservation?" Does not this weaken exegesis and the authoritative preaching of the Word of God? Personally speaking, this author has never seen even *one* MS of the Greek New Testament in more than thirty years of ministry,

---

[148] Glenney, 99.

and it is seriously doubted that many other preachers and students of God's Word have, either. Yet, colleges and seminaries teach their Greek students to do exacting work in the parsing of verb forms and conjugation of nouns. This would appear to be an exercise in futility if the text were in doubt. Why bother with the language nuances of word and tense significance if one has no assurance that he is parsing the appropriate word or form? And when applications for preaching are dependent upon precise exegesis, what happens to the authority of preaching when the text is in doubt?

Furthermore, what will happen when more MSS are discovered in the future? Will those who now use the W-H text maintain a "fluid" concept of God's Word? If a Greek MS from which the Syriac Peshitta was translated in 170 AD were to be discovered, would it then be considered "oldest and best" by those who now follow the Critical Text? Or, could future MS discoveries perhaps introduce a *third* major option for the critics? Given their system of thought, is it not plausible that a future discovery might rival the impact of "Sinaiticus" and "Vaticanus?" Will it become necessary for an entirely new "Revised Critical" text to be produced, exposing the "corruptions" in the 1881 text? If that happens, will a future generation of textual critics conclude that Fundamentalists in the twentieth century *did not have full access to God's preserved Word*?

It appears self-evident that the ministries of Fundamentalists today are built upon the *assumption* of the preservation of the text of Scripture. Such an assumption also seems to be characteristic of Bible-believers through Church history.

> The verbal inerrancy of Scripture has been the historic faith of the church in all ages. Some Liberal critics speak as though only a few "obscurantist Fundamentalists" would believe that Scripture is without error. On the contrary, scholarly believers from many different theological opinions in all periods of the church have treasured this faith in the Bible as the inerrant Word of God.[149]

The author of the preceding quotation, who is an advocate of the Critical Text, followed that statement with pronouncements by Clement of Rome, Irenaeus, Augustine, John Calvin, John Wesley, Martin Luther, and three modern writers to verify their affirmation of the inerrancy of Scripture.[150] It is the natural and logical assumption that the Scriptures which Irenaeus (who died about 202 AD) saw as inerrant were not different from the Scriptures that the Reformers and modern writers also saw as inerrant. Inerrancy, by definition, would demand that conclusion, and there is nothing in the quotations cited that would indicate otherwise. Since inerrancy has been the consistent belief

---

[149] Stewart Custer, Does Inspiration Demand Inerrancy? (Nutley, NJ: The Craig Press, 1968), 63.

[150] Ibid., 63-66.

throughout Church history, and since the only Greek text that has been available to man in all those periods has been the Traditional text, the *assumption* of preservation again points to the TR as the true text.

It seems, to this writer, that the real issues revolve around the teachings of Scripture and man's interpretation of historical information. At the risk of redundance, let it again be said that whether or not God has promised to make His Word available to all generations of mankind since its writing is a key issue. The position taken here is that He *has* so promised.

Furthermore, the way one *interprets* the facts of history (primarily seen through archaeological findings) will tend to direct him to one side of the debate or the other. As stated before, This writer has never had the privilege of seeing *even one* of the more than 5,600 extant Greek MSS, and it is suspected that many who have written or spoken vehemently about them have not either. Thus, there is a great deal of dependency upon the studies and observations of others. The view taken here is to accept the historical interpretations of those who have based their conclusions upon the belief that God has promised to preserve His Word. Thus, when men like John Burgon, Edward Miller, and Jakob Van Bruggen offer explanations that differ from Westcott and Hort's conclusions about the same phenomena, the choice here is made to follow Burgon and his supporters.

Both sides of the historical issue build arguments from items that have been *found* and from items that have *not been found, but are assumed to have existed.* They are often seen to differ in their interpretations of that which has been found, and they certainly disagree on that which they merely assume to have existed. In short, both seem to build their arguments partly from archeological and historical silence. At that point it becomes a *faith* issue, rather than one of clearly-demonstrable historical information. It need not be an unreasoned faith, however, but one that is based upon the Bible and logic. Since the TR has been rejected by critics primarily because "Syrian" MSS dating from the first few centuries have not been discovered, it must also be born in mind that the *autographa* (original writings) have not been discovered either! Yet no Bible-believer doubts that the *autographa* actually existed in history. The entire faith of Christians is founded upon that assumption. Likewise, the fact that earlier "Syrian" MSS have not been *found* does not mean that they *never existed.* It seems reasonable to conclude that they were worn out by constant use. For that reason, this writer has chosen to exercise his faith in agreement with those who defend a Biblical position on the preservation of Scripture. It should also be noted that faith does not denote that which is *uncertain*, but that which is simply *unseen.*

Regardless of what position Fundamentalists have taken on the textual issue, there is always the danger of allowing pride to dominate, hidden behind the mask of "conviction." Once an individual has publicly articulated his position (as in a sermon, lecture, book, or position paper), it becomes increasingly difficult to ever consider changing that position. Also, loyalties to denominations, institutions, and personalities further complicate the process of seeking the truth at all costs. This is a temptation that Fundamentalists must avoid. As Mr. Joel Spencer, one of this author's colleagues, has so succinctly stated, "It does not matter *who* is right; it matters *what* is right."

While many other scenarios might be imagined, the few mentioned here can be seen as sufficient to demonstrate the practical necessity of an agreed-upon text. Thankfully, in the Providence of God, such a text has been accessible for all of Church history. It is a text whose message has been powerfully and authoritatively proclaimed throughout the centuries. It is the Traditional, "Syrian," "Byzantine," *Textus Receptus*.

A Comparison of Textual Approaches

	"Faith" Approach	"Science" Approach
Biblical basis for verbal inspiration	II Tim 3:16; II Pet 1:21	II Tim 3:16; II Pet 1:21
Form of inspiration	Autographa	Autographa
Benefits of inspiration	Every word for lst generation	Every word for lst generation
Biblical basis for verbal preservation	Ps 33:11; Ps 119:89-90	Some say no Biblical basis, others disagree
Form of preservation	Copies of autographa	All extant MSS (changing number)
Benefits of preservation	Every word for future generations	Every word is *somewhere*
Biblical basis for textual accessibility	Isa 59:21; Lk 4:4	None
From of accessibility	Extant MSS	Missing for 400 yrs
Extent of accessibility	Every word for all	Limited to scholars
Biblical basis for choosing text	I Tim 3:15; Jude 3	None
Form of chosen texts	Byzantine MSS, TR	W-H Critical Text
Benefits of text chosen	*Assurance* that none is lost	*Probability* that little is lost

Chapter 12

Conclusion

To summarize the effort of this study, there are abundant Biblical, historical, and practical reasons to believe that God has preserved the New Testament portion of His Word in the Greek language of the *Textus Receptus,* but this issue should be debated lovingly among Fundamentalists, rather than dividing them from each other.

The Biblical evidence for preservation has several aspects. It is seen in the many New Testament quotations from and references to Old Testament passages. It is asserted numerous times in both Testaments, from the standpoints both of God's promise to preserve and man's need for such preservation. It is demonstrated in the two classic New Testament passages about the inspiration of Scriptures (II Tim 3:15-17 and II Pet 1:19-21), where both contexts also reveal that the Scriptures *had been precisely preserved*, even though the Hebrew autographa no longer existed. Important to the issue at hand are the Biblical charges to New Testament believers and local churches regarding their responsibility to the text. The New Testament seems to assign Church-age believers to be God's primary vehicle for the preservation of His Word.

History, then, continues the argument. It is incontrovertible that believers throughout the vast majority of recorded Church history have endorsed the TR tradition of the text. As for that small portion of history (the first three centuries) from which archaeologists have not discovered actual manuscript copies, the versions and Ante-Nicene Church fathers contribute evidence of the usage of the Traditional text. The pronounced dominance of the "Syrian" and "Byzantine" strain in the Post-Nicene era, the Middle Ages, and the Reformation period verify that the local churches were united in their desire to maintain and propagate the Traditional text. Since the local churches' practice concerning the *canonization* of Scripture is accepted as authoritative, so should be their practice concerning its *preservation.* And, since history must always be subservient to Scripture in authority, that historical interpretation (of Burgon and others) which accounts for the Biblical promise of preservation is accepted above one (of Westcott, Hort, and their followers) which questions accurate preservation.

From a practical standpoint, in order for believers to be able to evaluate their own obedience to *every word* of Scripture, they must *have* every word. For a student of the Bible to be properly motivated in precise exegesis of the New Testament, he must work with the text under the assumption that every prefix, suffix, stem change, preposition, and root word are precisely known. For a preacher to have Biblical authority in his preaching, he must not be in doubt regarding the text of Scripture. For the lost to be won to Christ, there must be no question about the accuracy of God's Word. But the real debate lies in the realm of the Greek texts used, rather than the KJV or any other translation of them. English-speaking people have no more legitimate exclusive claim upon God's truth than do those who speak Spanish, German, French, or any other language.

As important as all these issues are, it is also important, in the spirit of II Tim 2:24-25, that believers demonstrate courtesy toward each other in the debate. Since there are many Fundamentalists who hold differing views while still maintaining a commitment to the inspiration and inerrancy of the Scriptures, Bible-believers must not see *each other* as enemies. The battle is better fought when the *real* Enemy (Satan) is identified. The desire of this author is that these thoughts may stimulate more intelligent, gentlemanly debate among believers who desire to edify each other. May *issues*, rather than *personalities*, dominate the discussion, and may the Lord be pleased, not only with the Fundamentalist preacher's *position*, but also with his *disposition*.

WORKS CITED

Aland, Kurt, Matthew Black, Bruce M. Metzger, and Allen Wikgren, editors. The Greek New Testament. Stuttgart: Wurttemberg Bible Society, 1966.

Alexander, Pat, editor. The Lion Encyclopedia Bible. Lion Publishing Corporation, (reprinted by the Reader's Digest Association, Inc., 1987).

Arndt, William F., and F. Wilbur Gingrich. A Greek-English Lexicon of the New Testament. Chicago: the University of Chicago Press, 1952.

Burgon, John William. The Revision Revised, 1883. Collingswood, NJ: reprinted by The Bible for Today.

_____. The Traditional Text, 1896. Collingswood, NJ: reprinted by The Bible for Today.

Clark, Gordon H. Logical Criticisms of Textual Criticism. Jefferson, Maryland: The Trinity Foundation, 1986.

Cloud, David W., editor. "O Timothy Magazine." Volume 15, issues 3-4, 1998.

Custer, Stewart. Does Inspiration Demand Inerrancy? Nutley, NJ: The Craig Press, 1968.

________. The Truth About the King James Version Controversy. Greenville: Bob Jones University Press, Inc., 1981.

Glenny, W. Edward, in The Bible Version Debate: The Perspective of Central Baptist Theological Seminary. Minneapolis: Central Baptist Theological Seminary, 1997.

Harris, R. Laird, Gleason L. Archer, and Bruce K. Waltke, eds. Theological Wordbook of the Old Testament. Chicago: Moody Press, 1980, Volume I.

Kittel, Gerhard, editor. Theological Dictionary of the New Testament. Grand Rapids: Wm. B. Eerdmans Publishing Company, 1991, Volume I.

Ladd, George Eldon. The New Testament and Criticism. Grand Rapids: William B. Eerdmans Publishing Company, 1983.

Miller, Edward. A Guide to the Textual Criticism of the New Testament, 1886. Collingswood, NJ: reprinted by the Dean Burgon Society, Inc..

Miller, Edward, in the Preface to John William Burgon, The Traditional Text, 1896.

Nestle, Erwin, and Kurt Aland, eds. Novum Testamentum Graece. Stuttgart, Germany: Wurttembergischen Bibelenstalt Stuttgart, 24th edition, 1960.

Newman, Albert Henry. A Manual of Church History. Chicago: The American Baptist Publication Society, 1957, Volume I.

Pickering, Wilbur. The Identity of the New Testament Text. Nashville: Thomas Nelson Publishers, 1977.

Preface to The Dynamite of God: New American Standard Bible New Testament. New York: New York Bible Society, 1963.

Preface to The Holy Bible: Revised Standard Version. New York: Thomas Nelson & Sons, 1953.

Preface to The New Testament: the Old and New Versions on Opposite Pages. New York: Dodd, Mead & Company, 1881.

Shaylor, Randolph, editor. From the Mind of God to the Mind of Man. Greenville, SC: Ambassador-Emerald International, 1999.

Strouse, Thomas M. Fundamentalism and the Authorized Version. Virginia Beach, VA: Tabernacle Baptist Theological Press, 1996.

Thayer, Joseph Henry, editor. A Greek-English Lexicon of the New Testament. Edinburgh: T. & T. Clark, 1955.

Warfield, Benjamin B. An Introduction to the Textual Criticism of the New Testament. New York: Thomas Whittaker, 1886

Westcott, Brooke Foss, and John Anthony Hort. The New Testament in the Original Greek. New York: the MacMillan Company, 1928.

Van Bruggen, Jakob. The Ancient Text of the New Testament. Winnipeg: Premier Printing, Ltd., 1976.

12194080R00066

Printed in Great Britain
by Amazon.co.uk, Ltd.,
Marston Gate.